W9-APK-116
CHICAGO PUBLIC LIBRARY
HAROLD WASHINGTON LIBRARY CENTER
R0007241071

The Smallest Freezers

by the same author

COOK AHEAD (Macdonald)

NEVER TOO LATE (Macdonald)

WASTE NOT WANT NOT (Macdonald)

LEAVE IT TO COOK— new and revised edition (Penguin)

THE SMALLEST FREEZERS

and how to make the most of them

STELLA ATTERBURY

FABER AND FABER LIMITED
3 Queen Square London

First published in 1977
by Faber and Faber Limited
3 Queen Square London WC1
Printed in Great Britain by
Latimer Trend & Company Ltd Plymouth

British Library Cataloguing in Publication Data

Atterbury, Stella
The smallest freezers.
1. Food, Frozen—Amateurs' manuals
2. Home freezers
I. Title
641.4'53 TX610

ISBN 0-571-10888-1
ISBN 0-571-11176-9 Pbk

Contents

Introduction page 9

PART 1—FREEZING IN GENERAL—SMALL FREEZERS IN PARTICULAR

Freezers and Refrigerators 13
Then and Now 13
Small Freezers 13

How to Use Your Freezer 14
Hygiene 14
Freezing—General Principles 15
Block Freezing 16
Packaging 17
Stacking 21
Record Keeping 22
How Long Should Food Remain Frozen? 22
Foods That Should Not Be Frozen 24
Defrosting—Voluntary and Involuntary 24

Stocking Small Freezers 26

From Freezer to Table 30
How Should Frozen Food Be Thawed—Reheated—Cooked—Served? 30
From Freezer to Table in Under Thirty Minutes 38

PART 2—COOKING FOR OR FROM THE FREEZER

Ways and Means 43

Weights and Measures 43

Slow Cooking Method 44

The Recipes

Soup 47
Fish 49
Meat and Poultry 54
Light, Savoury and First Course Dishes 83
Vegetables, Salads and Herbs 106
Fruit 122
Puddings, Sweets, Sweet Sauces and Fillings 123
Cake Foundation—the Base for Cakes, Scones, Biscuits, Sponge Puddings, Sweet Short Pastry and Mock Lemon Curd 133
Pastry 151
Savoury Sauces 160
Cream and Custard 171
Yeast Cookery 175

Freezing Surplus Foods 181

Store-cupboard Supplements 183

Index 185

Figure—Preparation of Croissants 179

Introduction

Freezers of all sizes are installed in our homes now that we realize how much home freezing can improve our way of living.

When buying a freezer, we are often advised to get as large a one as possible; yet many of us find that the smallest is the best for our small homes.

This book is intended for the owners of these small freezers, with the hope that it will help them make the most use of every cubic inch of storage space and enjoy to the full the many advantages of home freezing.

PART 1
Freezing in General— Small Freezers in Particular

Freezers and refrigerators

Then and Now

Varied meals without waste or constant shopping depend largely on storage; therefore before refrigeration, a couple or anyone living alone could only buy or prepare small quantities of perishable foods. Refrigeration altered this and revolutionized catering. The variety of menus improved and the hours spent in the kitchen or at the shops were reduced. Today the majority of those who can afford a refrigerator consider it an essential adjunct to modern living.

For some years home freezers have also been with us. These initially were in the form of bulky chests, only suitable for large families with ample accommodation. Now that freezers come in all shapes and sizes, it's a very different story. There is a freezer to suit all households from the smallest to the largest. Yet how often we hear the plea 'A freezer for one or two is an unnecessary luxury'—a view which I and countless others either living alone or with small families consider unjustified. We realize that in our own way we benefit every bit as much from our very small freezers (packed with practical portions of a good variety of foods and prepared dishes) as the harassed mum or hostess with her enormous freezer stacked with the results of long cookery sessions and massive bulk buying. We can enjoy our own choice of à la carte meals and also save time, effort and cash. Single people who are out at work all day can, with the aid of a carefully stocked small freezer, sit down by themselves or with guests to either simple or exotic meals within 20–30 minutes of homecoming.

Small Freezers

The smallest freezers are made either to stand on top of a refrigerator or working surface or form part of a fridge-freezer. This means that almost every home that has room for a fridge can also house a freezer. These small freezers have a storage capacity of 1·5–2·5 cubic feet (42·5–63·5 litres) and accommodate about 40 to 62 lb (18–28 kilos) of food.

With experience and know-how, it's amazing how much food can be stored in what may appear limited space.

Before buying your small freezer you must choose between a free-standing one or a fridge-freezer. If you already have a satisfactory fridge there is no problem; you are sitting pretty—just buy a freezer. It's when you are starting from scratch that you have to weigh the pros and cons. The original purchase of the separate items may be a little higher, but by shopping around this can often be greatly reduced. According to the experts the difference in running costs is negligible. In my opinion the separate freezer and refrigerator have two important advantages: (1) The refrigerator's own frozen food storage compartment provides extra storage space which makes an appreciated annex to an overcrowded freezer; (2) When the freezer is defrosted, all the frozen contents can be temporarily housed in the fridge, set at its lowest temperature. On the other hand the fridge-freezer has the considerable advantage that the fridge does not require frequent defrosting.

How to Use Your Freezer

Hygiene

All food to be frozen must be in perfect condition and handled no more than necessary. The utensils used for preparing the food must be scrupulously clean. Even in ideal conditions some micro-organisms (bacteria) may be present in the food to be frozen. The freezing process will result in a reduction of these but will not kill them all. The normal hygiene precautions for handling fresh food should, of course, still prevail after the food has been taken from the freezer.

Freezing—General Principles

Home freezers are designed to operate at a temperature of 0° F (−18° C) to −13° F (−26° C). In some freezers the setting is static, in others it can be regulated, in which case you will find −5° F (−21° C) a good economic temperature.

All freezers are thermometrically controlled to maintain the set temperature. Obviously this will rise temporarily whenever the freezer door is opened, and even more so when unfrozen food is introduced. Help your freezer and save electricity by opening it as seldom and for as short periods as possible. Never in any 24 hours add fresh food in excess of 4–6 lb (1·8–2·8 kilos) or 10 per cent of your freezer's total storage capacity. Newly-introduced food should be separated from already frozen food and placed according to the freezer manufacturer's instructions. Only when completely frozen should it be stacked in its storage position.

Whether or not you make the most of every cubic inch of your freezer's storage space depends largely on the shape of the packages to be frozen. If possible, they should be rectangular, but not too many of them should be over 1½–2 in (4–5 cm) high, or when stacking they may not fit into available spaces. Rectangular parcels are achieved: (1) by block freezing (p. 16); (2) by freezing food in rectangular foil containers (p. 18); (3) by freezing food in polythene bags, using the method explained on p. 20. Soft foods that might be damaged by close packing should first be hardened on open trays before being wrapped and packed (p. 19). Never freeze food in round containers—they waste so much space.

Block Freezing

All liquids, foods cooked in liquid, and many other foods, such as purées and sauces, are suitable for block freezing.

CONTAINERS FOR BLOCK FREEZING

Containers are necessary for the initial freezing, but as these are not left in the freezer, only a limited assortment is required. They should be made of plastic or foil, so that the frozen block can be easily ejected. Many of the foods you buy come in containers that can be had free. At the time of writing, a soft vegetable margarine and a low fat spread are sold in rectangular ½ lb plastic containers. These are good for freezing small quantities of any foods and just right for single servings of prepared dishes. (For larger quantities, buy margarines that are sold in square 1 lb containers and ice cream packed in square and oblong containers of various sizes.) Then there are commercially frozen foods sold in foil containers which can be used again for home freezing. Plastic ice cube trays are the answer for food that is wanted in smaller quantities. If you have to buy a tray, get one with as large cubes as possible; the tray itself may be too big for your small freezer, but it can easily be cut in half.

HOW TO BLOCK FREEZE

Place the food to be frozen in suitable containers. Prepared dishes are best in blocks of 1, 2 or 3 servings which can be used as they are or combined to feed larger numbers. See that the liquid covers the solids in the case of fish, meat and poultry dishes that include sauce or gravy.

When really cold, cover the food, either by attaching the container lid or with a piece of clinging film, and freeze for about 12 hours. Blocks of food, such as sauces and creamed or mashed potatoes, which may be larger than will be wanted at one meal,

should, if firm enough, be marked into sections with the back of a knife before freezing, otherwise during the initial freezing.
After approximately 12 hours, remove container from the freezer. Carefully insert a round-ended knife between the sides of the block or cubes and the container. Reverse the container on to a sheet of clinging wrapping film. Press the bottom of the container with your warm hand, which may be enough to release the frozen block; if not, wring out a cloth in very hot water, wrap it round the container for a moment, press again, and if necessary tap the container on to your working surface.
Wrap the blocks closely in the film. Pack in polythene bags, label, seal and stack in freezer as soon as packed. (For packing methods and materials see below.) Always place food in the freezer as soon as it is packed.

Packaging

To keep the food in prime condition, correct packing before deep freezing is essential. The food, when quite cold, chilled, or not more than twelve hours after being initially frozen, must be enveloped in moisture/vapour-proof material and efficiently sealed, after as much air as possible has been expelled from the package, if necessary using a straw to suck it out, or even a stick of macaroni! Contact with air is one of the worst things that can happen to food during storage. It dehydrates the food, forms frost, and makes fat become rancid more quickly.
Liquid foods and prepared dishes with a high liquid content will expand when frozen. If they are packed in containers, half an inch head space must be left between the food and the container lid.

PACKING MATERIALS

As home freezing gains in popularity, new and improved packing materials appear on the market, making the choice ever wider. Here I can only give as a guide the materials that I consider best at the time of writing. You may find others that suit you better. However, make a point of buying those stipulated as being suitable for freezing. Remember that high-quality freezing depends on correct packaging. A considerable amount of money can be spent on these materials, especially when one first owns a freezer; yet as our small freezers are usually housed in small kitchens, one does not want to accumulate more requisites than necessary. This is my choice:

PACKING MATERIALS TO BUY

A roll of clinging film This is intended to cling to the food and itself. These films are re-usable if thoroughly washed, though they may lose much of their sealing quality. I find 'Stretch'n Seal' highly satisfactory, but there are several other makes on the market.

Polythene bags Made with gussets, specially for freezing and sold in packets. Two packets should be sufficient—sizes 4 × 8 × 2 in (10 × 20 × 5 cm) and 6 × 12 × 3 in (15 × 30 × 8 cm). These also are re-usable provided they are well washed and dried.

A roll of waxed paper This is not for wrapping food, but is useful for separating foods—such as pancakes (before they are wrapped) and for placing on top of food in foil containers.

Rectangular foil dishes They are useful for block freezing, especially those sold with separate lids (p. 15), and for storing prepared food which will require baking before serving. Freezer space will not be wasted provided the dishes are adequately filled. Food that was block frozen in foil containers can be returned to a like-sized container for its spell in the oven before serving. I find the most useful size 6⅜ × 4½ × 1 (16 × 11·5 × 2·5 cm).

RE-USING COMMERCIAL PACKING MATERIALS

More often than not food is sold wrapped or packed in materials that can be washed and re-used for home freezing. Brittle non-clinging cellophane is not suitable for freezing, but pliable film wrappings make good underwraps. Polythene bags in which food is purchased can be used for freezing. Use two if there is any doubt as to the correct thickness. Rectangular plastic or foil containers can be re-used for storing or block freezing (p. 16). Trays of expanded polystyrene are a gift to freezer owners. They are used widely for prepacked fruit, vegetables and other commercially packaged foods. They come in many sizes, and can be trimmed with kitchen scissors. (They are better for packaging without rims and with rounded corners.) If needed, two trays can be joined with paper clips to make one larger tray.

The flat trays can be slipped into polythene bags either with or without the food. They are also excellent for the initial open freezing of soft foods. They should be washed thoroughly before re-use.

PACKING ACCESSORIES

Special freezer tape This tape ensures the neatest packages. Used lengths need not be discarded. If wound on to an empty cotton reel, they can await future use. Keep a paper clip on the end of both new and used tape so that it does not stick tiresomely to the reel or to itself.

Paper or plastic-covered wire ties These seal polythene bags quickly but not as efficiently or neatly as the tape for rectangular packages. These ties are re-usable.

Elastic bands These may perish and are not really suitable for the freezer—certainly not for long-term storage—but they are quite satisfactory for fastening partially used packages which will shortly be finished.

Labelling It's surprising how quickly we forget the contents of frozen packages unless they are clearly marked. Special labels can be bought, but are unnecessary. Strips of thickish paper or thin cardboard, about 2 × ¾ in (5 × 2 cm), answer the purpose. In a few spare minutes you can cut strips of used envelopes, etc. to last for months. With a felt-tip pen, record the type of food, the quantity and the date of freezing. Slip the label inside the polythene bag before sealing.

HOW TO PACK RECTANGULAR PARCELS

A. Blocks of Frozen Foods

1. Underwrap the frozen block in the film on to which it has been ejected from its container (p. 17). To eliminate any air, ensure that the film closely contacts the block and clings to itself.
2. Put the wrapped block into a polythene bag, somewhat larger than itself, and lay it on a working surface, where it must remain until sealed.
3. Push the block to the bottom of the bag and insert the label.
4. Turn the corners of the bag opening towards each other, thus closing the bag with an angular end as with brown-paper parcels.
5. Press out any air and turn the folded end over the block. Temporarily weigh it down with anything handy, so that no air can penetrate before the freezer tape has sealed the parcel and fastened the bag opening into position.
6. Miniature blocks should be packed flat in the same way, not individually wrapped.

B. Food in Rectangular Foil Containers

Foil containers with their own lids No further wrapping is necessary, provided half an inch head space has been allowed between the food and the lid.

Foil containers without lids Place a piece of waxed paper over the food, slip the container into a polythene bag, a little bigger than itself, and lay it on a working surface, and continue as given for A 3, 4 and 5.

C. Dry Foods

Unless these are very awkwardly shaped they can be made into rectangular parcels if packed in polythene bags that are laid on a working surface. With some foods it helps if the bags are made rigid with polystyrene trays (p. 19).

Hard or reasonably hard foods These should be underwrapped in a clinging film before they are pushed to the bottom of the bag, again keeping the packet as square as possible.

Soft foods These should first be hardened by freezing in open trays before being underwrapped and put into bags.

Foods that pack compactly Foods such as peas and soft fruit do not need underwrapping (though some soft fruit, such as raspberries, should first be frozen in open trays). Spoon these foods into the bags, pushing them into the corners and expanding the gussets. Be very careful to remove as much air as possible. To seal bags, after inserting labels, continue as for A 4 and 5.

Stacking

The smaller the freezer the more important is the stacking of the frozen packages, and when these are rectangular, the maximum use of storage space is realized. However, it is one thing to fill the freezer to capacity and another to find a particular package, without dislodging a host of others. To start with, a shelf is essential. This is an integral part of many freezers, though the makers of some of the cheaper fridge-freezers save production costs by dispensing with shelves. Luckily this can be rectified with one of the plastic-covered metal shelves sold at most large ironmongers. But when a freezer is really full, even with a shelf, it is not easy to find and extricate a package without disturbing the rest. The answer to this problem is long plastic boxes, a little shorter than the freezer's depth and about 4 in (10 cm) wide. These are used without their lids to serve as do the wire baskets and trays in larger freezers. You can do with four of these boxes—two for the freezer bottom and two for the shelf. For records, it helps if the boxes are numbered. Try to keep each box for particular foods.

Record Keeping

Records that show at a glance just what your small freezer contains and where it can be found are invaluable and worth a little trouble. You don't need anything complicated like a card index, but can manage with a notebook or even a large sheet of paper ruled into columns for the different types of food. List the quantity of food in each package, the date of freezing and its position in the freezer. Don't forget to cross out items as they are used.

How Long Should Food Remain Frozen?

How long frozen food should remain in the freezer is a matter over which there is a considerable difference of opinion. The food could be left in the freezer indefinitely and would never go bad or be dangerous to eat. However, after a certain time it will deteriorate, eventually lose its flavour and texture and become inedible. Foods vary as to how long they can remain frozen before this deterioration begins. The experts agree on this, but not as to the number of weeks or months before the high-quality storage no longer pertains. The following chart gives the divergent opinions. Judge for yourself, but do not hoard frozen food; serve each item when it is still in its prime and will be most appreciated.

Recommended Approximate Storage Times (in months)

FOOD IN FREEZER	APPROXIMATE MAXIMUM STORAGE
BREAD and CAKES	
Bread: Plain	1–12
Rich	3
Risen Dough	2– 3
Cakes: Undecorated	3– 6
Iced	2
DAIRY PRODUCE	
Butter: Salted	3– 6
Unsalted	6–12
Margarine and Lard	5–12
Cheese: Cream	3– 6
Hard	6
Cottage	3– 4
Milk, Homogenized	1– 3
Cream	2– 6
Eggs	10–12
FISH	
Cod, Whiting, Sole, Plaice	6–12
Halibut, Mackerel, Herring, Trout, Salmon	3– 8
Crab, Lobster, Prawns, Shrimps:	
Uncooked	3–10
Cooked	1–10
Oysters, Scallops	1–10
Smoked Fish	1–10
FRUIT and VEGETABLES	
Fruit: Without Sugar	6–12
With Sugar or Syrup	9–12
Purée	6– 8
Juices	4– 6
Vegetables	9–12

FOOD IN FREEZER	APPROXIMATE MAXIMUM STORAGE
ICE CREAM	1– 3
MEAT and POULTRY, UNCOOKED	
Joints: Beef, Lamb	8–12
Pork, Veal	4–6
Chops and Escalopes: Lamb, Pork, Veal	3– 4
Minced Meat	1– 3
Offal	2– 6
Sausages: Seasoned	1– 4
Unseasoned	3– 8
Ham and Bacon Cuts	2– 4
Bacon Rashers	1– 4
Poultry and Game	6–12
Chicken Livers	3
COOKED MEAT and POULTRY	
Roast Meat and Poultry	2– 6
Sliced Left-overs	1
Casseroled Dishes	3– 4
Meat Pies	3– 4
Meat Loaves, Balls and Fried Meat	2– 3
Dishes Made from Left-over Meat and Poultry	1
PASTRY	
Doughs, shaped or in bulk	6
Pies: Baked	6
Unbaked	3
SOUPS and SAUCES	2– 4

Foods That Should Not Be Frozen

Green salad plants, cucumber (except when frozen in dressing), bananas, hard-boiled eggs, custard pies, soft meringue, mayonnaise and sour or single cream (except when used as an ingredient), carbonated drinks should not be frozen. Apart from these you can safely experiment and freeze small quantities of almost any food that attracts you. There is no danger that freezing can make unquestionably fresh food harmful.
Garlic is a controversial ingredient. Some pundits say it loses its flavour after freezing, others that it adopts an unpleasant flavour. My family and I have no complaint after dishes containing it have been a month or so in the freezer, and happily use it in our short-stay casseroles.
There are, however, flavours, such as vanilla essence (vanilla pods and vanilla sugar are all right) and cloves, that become too strong with freezing. These should be avoided unless the dish is to be served in the near future.

Defrosting—Voluntary and Involuntary

VOLUNTARY DEFROSTING

This should take place when the frost and ice, which accumulate on the freezer's coldest surfaces, have reached a thickness of ¼ in (1 cm). This situation can be considerably postponed if some of the frost deposit is regularly removed by scraping (say every 15 to 20 days) with a plastic spatula, never a metal one. The electricity need not be switched off, and only if the freezer is crowded will it be necessary to remove a few packages for a short time.
Try to synchronize full-scale defrosting with a reasonably empty freezer. First turn off the electricity supply and remove all the frozen food. This is an occasion when a separate freezer is appreciated, because the food can be stacked in the fridge, set at its coldest. In the

case of fridge-freezers, except for the larger models, the motor is shared and the fridge as well as the freezer will be switched off; therefore the food should preferably be put into an insulated bag or otherwise wrapped compactly in a thick layer of newspapers with a blanket round the lot and stored in a cool place.

Defrosting can be accelerated if several small bowls of warm, not hot, water are placed in the open freezer, or a hand-held hair drier is directed on to the freezer's ice-covered surfaces. To save a lot of mopping up, try to remove the ice as it loosens, with the help of a plastic spatula. When clear, wipe freezer with a solution of warm water and bicarbonate of soda. Dry well. Turn on current, but do not return frozen packages until it has been running for 1–2 hours, and do not put in unfrozen food for at least a further 2 hours.

INVOLUNTARY DEFROSTING

This may take place for different reasons—a power failure, a blown fuse, or carelessness. If a freezer's electricity supply has been cut off, no harm will come to its frozen contents for up to 24 hours, *provided the door has not been opened.*

Many of the larger freezers have a warning light or bell to indicate a failed power supply. With our small freezers we are at a disadvantage. We may or may not be aware of a power cut, but are unlikely to discover a blown fuse or a faulty or inadvertently turned-off switch, until we have opened our freezer and realize the trouble. We must then quickly close the door, ascertain the cause of the failure, and put it right if we can. Take a power cut calmly—they are not usually of long duration. The freezer must not be opened again until the power has been restored for two hours, when the condition of the contents should be checked.

All foods that are only partially thawed and still contain ice crystals may be refrozen.

Raw meat, fish and poultry that has only just thawed and is still very cold and firm to the touch may be treated as normally thawed food and cooked either for immediate consumption of for refreezing in a cooked state. This does not apply to vegetables, dairy produce or pre-cooked dishes which should be discarded.

Foods that are completely thawed are a different story. We just don't know how long they have been in that condition and should take no risks and discard them. Fruit, bread and cakes (without cream fillings) are the only exceptions. If the fruit looks and tastes all right it may be made into a pureé or sauce. Bread and cakes, provided there is no musty smell, may be refrozen.

Stocking Small Freezers

Apart from bought commercially frozen food, prepared seasonal food and dishes for special occasions, the stocking of small freezers can become automatic by adopting the following practice.
Each time food that would be appreciated in the weeks and months ahead is prepared for today, make at least twice as much as is needed. The surplus can be frozen either before or after it has been cooked, according to the recipe.
Our freezers are our larders for perishable foods and prepared dishes, and the smaller these freezers are, the more selective we must be as to their contents. We should fill them with as varied and as space-saving a choice as possible. It is hoped that the following suggestions may help to achieve that aim.

Soup

Soup is not only valuable in itself, but as a means of making excellent use of surplus foods. Yet how often we are lumbered with these left-overs when we either do not want soup or have no time to make it. With a freezer, however small, there is no need to worry. You can either block freeze the surplus food until soup is on your menu or make the soup in a concentrated form, adding the extra liquids when the block is heated and served (p. 47).

Fish

Uncooked fish Unless you catch your own or live near the source of supply, packets of commercially frozen fillets and steaks are the best buy for freshness and possibly cost too.

Cooked fish dishes These are easy to prepare and better value than commercially frozen fish dishes. However, except for a few dishes—such as fish cakes, kedgeree and complicated dishes made for an imminent party—they are more satisfactory when made as required with frozen fish. Freezer space is saved and the dishes take little longer to prepare and cook (especially if made with a frozen sauce) than frozen cooked dishes take to thaw and reheat.

Meat and Poultry

Uncooked meat and poultry These freeze well, but are often awkwardly shaped and waste valuable freezer space. Owners of small freezers may therefore prefer to buy these as they are needed. Thinly cut steaks and veal fillet are exceptions—they need very little space and can be served within 20 minutes of leaving the freezer. Some people may also feel inclined to give space to trimmed chops or cutlets.

Prepared meat and poultry dishes Meat and poultry dishes are good inmates for all sizes of freezers. They keep their quality and need little space, providing any bones are removed before freezing.

Fruit, Vegetables and Herbs

The smallest freezer stocked with a selection of commercially frozen fruit and vegetables will ensure a constant and often out-of-season supply of garden produce. It is not worth buying this from the greengrocer and freezing it yourself except in the case of fruits and vegetables that are not commercially frozen but do freeze well.
Those who grow their own fruit and vegetables, even in a small way, would undoubtedly find a little freezer frustrating and in-

adequate. However, those town dwellers who spend weekends with family and friends in the country will de delighted with the ability to conserve their rural spoils (pp. 106 and 122).
Fresh herbs are easy to freeze. They retain their flavour for months and need little freezer space (p. 121).

Bread and Cakes

Most people enjoy freshly baked bread and cakes. If these are frozen either as soon as cool enough after emerging from the oven, or when bought very fresh from the baker, they will retain those delicious newly baked qualities, even after weeks in the freezer. The only drawback is the space they monopolize, but room can often be found for a few rolls, a loaf and a cake, especially when home-made. Also, Cake Foundation may be found a solution to fresh, quickly produced cakes (p. 133).
Those who often make sandwiches may like to freeze a small cut loaf. Sandwiches made with frozen slices should be just right for eating by the time they are wanted. Frozen cut loaves are also useful for toast.

Puddings and Sweets

Those who like puddings and sweets and can indulge in extra calories, will welcome as large a variety as freezer space allows. Custard pies, soft meringue and jellies are not satisfactory.

Pastry Dishes, Pastry Cases, Pastry Doughs

Unbaked or baked pastry dishes freeze well. Unbaked for choice except for the Quiche Lorraine type of flan.

Flan, tartlet or vol-au-vent cases, pastry slices and pie lids frozen flat and unbaked (pp. 157–60) are most successful and take up very little space.
Frozen blocks of pastry dough are useful, but must be thawed for an hour or so before they can be used.

Pancakes

Freezer owners usually find pancakes can provide the basis for many quick and interesting dishes—savoury or sweet (pp. 97 and 125).

Sauces

Haute cuisine relies partly on creating the right sauce for each dish and having a good selection of these sauces available gives the cook confidence and status. Without a freezer, the problem, especially when catering for small households, was that most recipes produce far more sauce than needed; therefore to avoid waste, each sauce had to be used up before a new one was made. Now we can produce sauces as wanted and freeze any surplus into small blocks. Thus in a short time a good selection of sauces which need little freezer space is acquired.

Milk and Cream

A little reserve milk in the freezer is a good idea for those who are often away from home. Homogenized milk packed in waxed cartons is the best buy (p. 23). Double or whipping cream with 40 per cent fat content freeze well (p. 171).

Coffee Beans

If you don't live near a good coffee shop, it is difficult always to make coffee with freshly roasted beans. This problem need not arise if whenever beans are bought, all but those required for immediate use are frozen in small polythene bags. Pack in each bag the normal amount used; then, when needed, grind the still frozen beans and enjoy that lovely aroma of freshly ground freshly roasted coffee beans.

Perishable Ingredients to Keep on Tap

The lack of one or more of these ingredients can often frustrate the inclination to prepare a particular dish. A constant supply will not take up much freezer space and is sure to prove useful. I like to keep a small amount of the following in my freezer: sliced onion, sliced carrot, sliced red or green pepper, sticks of celery, sliced lemon, grated cheese, rashers of green bacon or bacon pieces (derinded), fresh white breadcrumbs.

Left-overs

The freezer is a safe haven for left-overs, including the contents of partly used tins (p. 181). Lodged in the freezer, there's no need to decide straight away on their final role. Also delectable dishes prepared from recent left-overs can be stored until their origin is forgotten.

From Freezer to Table

How Should Frozen Food Be Thawed—Reheated—Cooked—Served?

There are different ways of thawing, cooking or reheating frozen foods. Some foods need a particular method, whereas others respond equally well to alternative methods which can be used as is convenient.

The following chart should prove a useful guide, but only a rough guide, as most of the given times must be approximate. This is inevitable, as the temperature of the frozen foods, refrigerators, rooms and oven settings is bound to vary to some extent.

FOOD	
Bread	
Loaves	SLOW METHODS Bread frozen when fresh, thawed in its freezer wrapping in the fridge or at room temperature will taste as if a day old. *In the fridge* leave overnight. *At room temperature* loaves 2–3 hours, French bread 1–2 hours. QUICK METHOD Bread thawed quickly in the oven is deliciously crusty and tastes as if freshly baked. The snag is, it quickly becomes stale and should be eaten there and then. Place in cold oven, set 350° F—180° C—Mark 4. Bake loaves 30–40 minutes, French bread 15–20 minutes.
Rolls	Rolls for immediate use should be placed in cold oven set 350° F—180° C—Mark 4 and baked 15–20 minutes.
Sliced bread	SLOW METHOD 1–2 hours at room temperature. QUICK METHOD A few minutes under a very low grill. Frozen slices can be toasted, fried, or used for making sandwiches. Slices can be cut off frozen loaves, but only with the right kind of knife, and then some loaves are more of a job than others, according to their density.
Par-baked rolls	Place rolls on floured tray and bake in pre-heated oven, 450° F—230° C—Mark 8 until browned.
Butter	Thaw for at least 2 hours, preferably longer, at room temperature.
Cakes	SLOW METHOD Cakes keep fresh longer when left in freezer wrappings and thawed at room temperature.
Undecorated	*Large cakes* at least 2 hours. *Small cakes* 30 minutes.

FOOD	
Cakes—*cont.*	QUICK METHOD For immediate use, cakes may be thawed (wrapped in cooking film or foil) in a preheated oven, 375° F—190° C—Mark 5. *Large cakes* 20–40 minutes. *Small cakes* 8–15 minutes.
Slices	Wrapped slices can be thawed at room temperature in about 1½ hours. Sponges can be sliced while still frozen.
Iced	Iced cakes must be thawed at room temperature either in loosened wrappings, which must not contact the cake's surface, or unwrapped in an airtight container.
Cheese	
Hard	Thaw in wrappings preferably in the fridge but, if necessary, at room temperature for 1½–2 hours.
Soft and cottage	A little cream can be mixed with cottage cheese, if it becomes crumbly after freezing.
Cream	Thaw at room temperature for 1–2 hours, or, if needed quickly, break up block and place on the bottom of a dish standing in a larger dish of very hot water. As soon as the cream begins to melt, crush with a fork and then beat gently.
Eggs	See p. 182.
Fish	
Wet or smoked (uncooked)	Fish—if not too large—may be boiled, steamed, grilled or fried as soon as it comes out of the freezer. Large fish, fish to be coated with egg and crumbs or batter, and fish to be baked, should be thawed or partially thawed before cooking. Wet fish, except

FOOD	
Fish—*cont.*	salmon, should be thawed in its wrapping. Salmon and smoked fish should be thawed unwrapped. Complete thawing of 1 lb fish requires 6 hours in the fridge or 3 hours at room temperature. When needed quickly, fish may be unwrapped and thawed in cold water. *Cook fish as soon as thawed.*
Shell fish (cooked)	To serve cold, thaw in unopened container: *In the fridge* 8 hours. *At room temperature* 4–6 hours.
Shell fish (uncooked)	Remove frozen shell fish from container or wrappings and plunge immediately into a pan of boiling water or court bouillon.
Oysters (raw)	Serve while still chilled and containing a few ice crystals.
Fish dishes (cold)	Thaw in the fridge, still wrapped, up to 24 hours.
Fish dishes (hot)	See pp. 52–4.
Fish cakes	Place fish cakes while still frozen or just beginning to thaw in a frying pan containing plenty of hot fat, over moderate heat. Allow about 5 minutes each side to brown and heat.
Fruit	
Frozen with or without sugar	Fruit should be served before it has completely thawed, whilst it still contains a few ice crystals. Though it takes so long, thawing in the fridge is preferable. To thaw 1 lb (400 g) fruit allow approximately (according to the density of the pack): *In the fridge* 6–9 hours. *At room temperature* 2–4 hours. When a small quantity is wanted quickly, spread it out on the bottom of a dish, placed in a larger dish of hot water and gently rotate with a fork.

FOOD	
Fruit—*cont.*	
Frozen in its own sweetened juices	To thaw 1 lb (400 g) fruit allow approximately: *In the fridge* 6–9 hours. *At room temperature* 2–4 hours. In an oven dish placed in a very cool oven 1 hour. Purées will take 50 per cent longer.
Ice cream	Ice cream should not be served directly from the freezer but should first spend about ¼ to 1 hour (depending on the type and quantity) in the fridge, 4–6 hours in the fridge frozen food storage compartment, or 10–15 minutes at room temperature.
Meat, raw	
Joints or thick cuts	It is essential that, before cooking, joints and thick cuts are completely thawed as slowly as possible. This not only ensures the thorough cooking of the centre of the joint but also the retention of meat juices. Thaw meat in freezer wrappings. Allow at least 9 hours per lb (400 g) in the fridge or approximately 3–5 hours per lb (400 g) at room temperature or in a cool larder. Joints can be thawed more quickly if, still wrapped, they are placed in frequent changes of cold water.
Steaks, chops or meat slices	Thaw, in freezer wrapping, in fridge for about 3 hours or at room temperature for 1½ hours. This or partial thawing is necessary when the meat is to be coated with egg and crumbs or dusted with flour. Otherwise, if more convenient, these cuts may be cooked while still frozen, provided only gentle heat is applied until the meat has entirely thawed.
Sausages	As above. Be sure to cook thoroughly.
Liver	Thick pieces or slices to be coated with egg and crumbs or dusted with flour should be thawed, unwrapped, in the fridge 3 hours, at room temperature 1½ hours.

FOOD	
Meat,—*cont.*	Thin slices, including those coated with egg and crumbs before freezing, may be cooked when frozen—provided only gentle heat is applied until the liver has thawed.
Meat, cooked	
Sliced, without sauce or gravy	Leave in freezer wrappings and thaw in the fridge or at room temperature. This can be served as cold meat or used in recipes that require cooked meat.
Joints	Remove from freezer at least a day before serving. Loosen wrappings and thaw in the fridge, at least 9 hours per l lb (400 g).
Casseroles and other meat dishes with sauce	Unless dish was frozen in a foil container, transfer it from its freezer packing to an oven dish or a heavy saucepan or, if the casserole contains egg yolks or cream, the top of a double saucepan or a basin that fits over a saucepan. OVEN METHOD Place dish, uncovered, in a cold oven set 350° to 375° F—180° to 190° C—Mark 4 to 5. Cook until completely heated—about 1–1½ hours per lb; an occasional gentle stir with a wooden spoon accelerates the process. If thawed, place dish in preheated oven for about 15–20 minutes. SAUCEPAN METHOD Place saucepan over gentle heat or in the case of a double saucepan or basin, over a saucepan of boiling water. Stir frequently with a wooden spoon until the dish has thawed, then now and then until it is really hot.
Fried meat	Remove from freezer wrappings and place on a baking tin. Cook for 15–20 minutes, according to the thickness of the meat, in pre-heated oven, 375° to 400° F—190° to 200° C—Mark 5 to 6.
Grilled sausages	Remove from freezer wrappings and place in grill pan. Thaw and reheat under low grill.
Milk	Thaw at room temperature for 6–8 hours.

FOOD	
Pastry	
Pastry dough	This, in freezer wrappings, should be thawed at room temperature only enough to enable rolling and shaping. This shaped dough must either be baked or refrozen while still ice-cold.
Uncooked rolled and shaped dough, pies, sausage rolls, pasties, etc.	Remove from wrappings and place on cold baking sheet in a cold oven, set as follows: *short crust,* 400° F—200° C—Mark 6; *flaky,* 475° F—245° C—Mark 9; *puff,* 450° F—230° C—Mark 8. Bake as if unfrozen but allow up to 10 minutes longer, reducing the heat if necessary.
Cooked pastry dishes	*To be served cold* thaw in wrappings in the fridge for at least 6 hours. *To be served hot* thaw and heat in oven 400° F—200° C—Mark 6 for about 25 minutes.
Poultry, uncooked	It is essential that frozen birds and poultry joints are completely thawed before they are cooked; not only because of the high risk of bacteria in uncooked poultry, but because the flavour is far better. Thaw in their wrappings. *In the fridge* birds (not over 4 lb (2 kg)) up to 24 hours, joints 6 hours. *At room temperature* birds 8–12 hours, joints 3 hours. Poultry can be thawed more quickly if, still wrapped, it is placed in frequent changes of cold water. Once thawed, poultry may be kept in the fridge for up to 24 hours—no longer.
Poultry, cooked	As given for cooked meat.

FOOD	
Sauces and soups	Transfer frozen block to a heavy saucepan and place over gentle heat. Stir continuously until about half the block has thawed and then frequently until the complete block has thawed. If the sauce or soup contains neither egg yolk nor cream, the heat may be raised. If, on the contrary, it does incorporate either of these ingredients (or if frequent stirring is not convenient), pour it into the top of a double saucepan over boiling water or into a basin that fits over a saucepan of boiling water.
Vegetables	BOILING All vegetables, except corn-on-the-cob, should be boiled while frozen (corn-on-the-cob should first be thawed at room temperature for 3–4 hours). For each 1lb (400 g) of vegetables allow ¼–½ pint (125–250 ml) salted water. Bring this to a rapid boil in a pan large enough to accommodate the vegetables. Add the vegetables and, when the water has returned to the boil, reduce heat and cook until just tender, allowing about half the time given to fresh vegetables. STEAMING Vegetables other than spinach should be partially thawed and separated before steaming. FRYING Gently fried frozen vegetables are delicious. Melt a knob of butter in a heavy covered pan. Add the frozen vegetables and seasoning. Lower the heat. Cook till tender, occasionally shaking pan or tossing vegetables with a fork. If there is too much liquid from the vegetables, let this evaporate by removing the pan lid shortly before they are cooked. OVEN COOKING Place partially thawed vegetables in a well-greased casserole with seasoning and a large knob of butter. Very little or no water is needed. Cover, and place in preheated oven 350° F—180 °C —Mark 4 and cook 30–40 minutes. Frequently shake casserole or toss vegetables with a fork.

FOOD	
Veg.—*cont.*	Completely thawed corn-on-the-cob is good when individually wrapped in buttered transparent baking wrap or foil and baked 30–40 minutes, oven 375° F—190° C—Mark 5.
Cooked vegetables or vegetable dishes	Thaw and heat as given for Cooked Meat Casseroles (p. 35).
Vegetable salads	See p. 120.

From Freezer to Table in Under Thirty Minutes

The preceding chart shows that many frozen foods and prepared dishes can be served in less than 30 minutes. No matter how small your freezer, if it is stocked with a varied selection of these, you can quickly produce interesting meals for most occasions. They can often be improved with refrigerator and store-cupboard support. This quickly served food is particularly useful for unexpected guests, and is appreciated by those who come home tired and hungry and fancy something more exciting than their fridge or larder can offer. It is much quicker to thaw and heat frozen food than just to thaw it, unless emergency methods are used.

Foods to be served cold are best thawed in the fridge or at room temperature, which takes considerably longer than 30 minutes. (Quicker emergency methods are much more trouble.) With this in mind, it is wise to make up your 30-minute à la carte menus mainly with hot dishes.

SOME QUICKLY SERVED FROZEN FIRST COURSE AND MAIN DISHES

(Those marked ★ are suitable for special occasions)

Soup (p. 47)
Fried or Grilled Fish (p. 49)
Fish Cakes (p. 51)
Kedgeree (p. 52)
Simmered Beef and Vegetables (p. 54)
★Flemish Braised Steak (p. 55)
★Smothered Steak (p. 56)
★Boeuf Bourgignonne (p. 57)
Hungarian Goulash (p. 58)
★Minute Steaks (p. 60)
Mince Minute Steaks and Onion (p. 60)
Chilli-con-Carne (p. 61)
Hamburgers (p. 62)
Swedish Meat Balls (p. 63)
★Lamb à la Manchèga (p. 64)
Bredee (p. 65)
★Hungarian Lamb (if sour cream is available) (p. 66)
Breast of Lamb Cutlets (p.68)
★Porc à la Fermière (p. 69)
★Chinese Sliced Pork (p. 70)
★Barbecued Spare Rib (p. 71)
★Veal with Mushrooms and Cream Sauce (p. 72)
★Wiener Schnitzel (p. 73)
★Pot Roast Venison (p. 75)
Fried Liver and Bacon Potato Cakes (pp. 76 and 89)
★Lambs' Kidneys à la Señorita (p. 77)
Chicken and Rice (p. 78)
★Fried Chicken à l'Espagnol (p. 79)
★Chicken Marengo (p. 80)
Curried Chicken (p. 81)
★Pigeons with Mushrooms or Peppers, Cooked in Sherry (p. 82)
Eggs Soubise (p. 84)
Curried Eggs (p. 84)
Cheese Aigrettes (p. 85)
Rarebits—Welsh, Buck and Celery (p. 87)
Cheese Pancakes (p. 87)
Cheese Eggs (p. 88)
Croque Monsieur (p. 88)
Bacon and Onion Roll (p. 90)
Quiche Lorraine (p. 92)
Grilled Sausages (p. 93)
Sausage Pinwheels (p. 93)
Sausage Rolls (p. 94)
Cornish Pasties (p. 95)
Curry Puffs (p. 95)
Filled Pancakes (p. 97)
Miniature Pancakes (p. 98) or Bouchées (p. 158) with Haddock or other Savoury Fillings (pp. 101–4)
Spaghetti Bolognese (p. 99)
Filled Pastry Cases (p. 101 and 157)
Pizza (p. 180)

VEGETABLES, POTATOES AND SALADS

Any commercially or home frozen vegetables, vegetable or potato dishes that you may have in your freezer (pp. 106–20) will be ready to serve well within 30 minutes.
For salads see p. 120.

SWEETS

Ice Cream and the many attractive ways in which it can be served (pp. 126–8) are the obvious answer for cold sweets. Those who do not favour ice cream can rely on Fresh Fruit Salad (p. 131) or tinned fruit. These should be served with Cream (p. 172) or Custard Cream (p. 174).
When a hot sweet is wanted, frozen Pancakes are the quickest to heat (pp. 97–8) and can be served in a number of ways (pp. 125 and 129–30). Provided a cooler oven is not wanted for reheating the main dish, frozen Puff Pastry Slices and filled Vol-au-Vent Cases are also good hot sweets (pp. 158–60).

BREAD STICKS

A few Bread Sticks (p. 177), apparently freshly baked, add a welcome finishing touch to any meal.

PART 2

Cooking for or from the Freezer

Ways and Means

As the great majority of foods can be successfully frozen and as most freezer owners already have their favoured recipes and cook books, special recipes for freezing (ices excepted) are not strictly needed. What is necessary is the knowledge of how the different foods should be treated before and after freezing, also the few foods that should not be frozen at all (p. 24). It is hoped that the advice given will prove helpful and that some of the dishes will share your freezer with favourites of pre-freezer days. Some of them are recipes in their own right, others are an amalgamation of foods from the freezer, sometimes joined by others from the fridge or store cupboard. Do remember that you are rarely obliged to cook especially for the freezer if, when preparing food for immediate serving, you make at least twice as much as is needed, so that the surplus food can be frozen. Another way to save time and effort is to use the Slow Cooking Method when applicable (p. 44).

Weights and Measures

Many of us grudge the abolition of our familiar British weights and measures, but the metric system is here and come to stay. The exact metric equivalent to the British would be awkward and impractical for daily use. For instance, try to work out a recipe with the correct assumption that 1 British oz = 28·35 g (grams).
To make life easier the powers that be have given us the following approximate metric conversions.

British		*Metric*
1 oz	=	25 g
$\frac{1}{4}$ lb (4 oz)	=	100 g
$\frac{1}{2}$ lb (8 oz)	=	200 g
1 lb (16 oz)	=	400 g
1 teaspoon ($\frac{1}{6}$ fluid oz)	=	5 ml (millilitres)
1 dessertspoon ($\frac{1}{3}$ fluid oz)	=	10 ml
1 tablespoon (just over $\frac{1}{2}$ fluid oz)	=	15 ml
1 fluid oz	=	25 ml
$\frac{1}{4}$ pint (5 fluid oz)	=	125 ml
9 fluid oz	=	$\frac{1}{4}$ litre (2·5 dl) (decilitres)
$\frac{1}{2}$ pint	=	250 ml
18 fluid oz	=	$\frac{1}{2}$ litre (5 dl)
1 pint	=	500 ml
$1\frac{3}{4}$ pints (35 fluid oz)	=	1 litre

As these convenience conversions are approximate, the metric dishes will weigh slightly less than their British counterparts. However, the relative weights and measures of the different ingredients will be more or less correct; therefore it is important that either the British or the metric system should be used consistently throughout a recipe. Cooks using the metric system will find it invaluable to have a set of metric measuring spoons (which are slightly smaller than the ordinary standard spoons) and a measure marked with millilitres for both dry and liquid ingredients.

Slow Cooking Method

This method enables a single, several, or a wide assortment of dishes to be cooked at one time in a very cool oven or one dish in a slow-cooking electric casserole. Ultra slow cooking is excellent for the many foods which benefit from never boiling or reaching a temperature that dries up the natural juices.

For many years I have been a keen follower of this method and have written a book on it—*Leave it to Cook* (Penguin).* Today, with a small freezer as well as a fridge, I find slow cooking even more valuable. Whereas in the old days the cooked dishes had to be eaten within a week, now they can be stored in the freezer and need not be served for months.

The ideal temperature for the Slow Cooking Method is:

electricity: over 180° F (82° C) under 200° F (93° C)
gas: Mark Low or 'S'†
Aga or Esse cookers: the simmering oven

Some cookers are not set lower than 200° F (93° C) or gas Mark ¼, which is a little too hot. However, cookers will often function slightly lower than the lowest given setting.

In all events, before slow cooking can be fully enjoyed, a spell of trial and error will be necessary so that the cook, the cooker and the method can adjust themselves to each other. The first time it is tried, set the oven at 180° F (82° C) or gas 'S' or Low. If the cooker does not register as low as that, set it at the lowest at which it will function. Put in one or two simple trial dishes and leave them for about 8 hours. If after that time the food is cooked to perfection, you have established the right setting for your slow cooking.

If the food is undercooked give it a little longer at a slightly higher temperature, and next time you experiment use a slightly higher setting in the first place.

If on the other hand your first setting proves too hot for slow cooking, the food will have simmered and be somewhat overcooked. Try a lower setting, if possible; otherwise you must follow choice (2) given below.

However long food is left in a very slow oven it will never burn or be ruined. The reason being that once food reaches the temperature of the oven in which it has been placed, it cannot get any hotter.

* New and revised edition.

† Gas cookers with an 'S' thermostat setting correct for the Slow Cooking Method are now manufactured by Flavel/Leisure.

Food left in an oven perfectly adjusted to slow cooking may have been cooked well before the 8 hours were up, but will come to no harm when left for the full time. This gives owners of ovens amenable to the Slow Cooking Method two choices:

(1) To leave the food to cook for 8 hours or more.
(2) To inspect the food periodically after the first 4–6 hours of cooking and remove any dishes that are cooked.

Some of us don't fancy a lot of early morning cooking. Luckily this need not arise, as most slow-cooked dishes can be made oven-ready well in advance of cooking and stored in the fridge until convenient. Of course, if preferred, choice (1) can be carried out throughout the night.

Many people's first reaction to the Slow Cooking Method is the fear of increased fuel bills. This need not be so, provided the oven is filled to capacity. In fact there may be a small saving in costs and there will be a considerable saving of time and energy when, after hours of unsupervised cooking, a nice hot meal ready to eat straight away, together with a selection of dishes for the weeks ahead, emerges from the oven.

Careful stacking is necessary so that your oven will accommodate the greatest variety of dishes.

The temperature in ovens (other than fan-heated ovens), whatever the settings, varies slightly according to the shelf position. The hottest part in all ovens is the top shelf. The coolest in all gas and some electric ovens is the bottom, though in the latter it is sometimes the centre. Experience will soon show which positions the different dishes prefer in your oven. The oven floor can be used for slow cooking in many electric ovens, but is usually not hot enough in gas cookers.

FOODS AMENABLE TO ULTRA-SLOW COOKING AND DEEP FREEZING

Meat, poultry and game They are first in this category, led by casseroled dishes. These surpass themselves when cooked in the medium or hottest position of a very cool oven.

Cereal and milk dishes, sweet and savoury Milk puddings, when cooked covered in the hottest position of a very slow oven, could not be creamier. All the cream remains in the pudding and is not wasted in the skin. The homely rice pudding is transformed into a delicious creamed rice.

Egg, milk and bread dishes, savoury or sweet Cooked uncovered at medium or hot position in the very cool oven.

Fried rice This can be left to cook in an ultra-slow oven (p. 105).

Fruit These are excellent when slow cooked in a covered container with sweetening but no water (pp. 122–3). The one process produces firm, cooked fruit in its own syrup.

RECIPES PARTICULARLY SUITABLE FOR THE SLOW COOKING METHOD

Flemish Braised Steak (p. 55)
Boeuf Bourguignonne (p. 57)
Hungarian Goulash (p. 66)
Hamburgers (p. 62)
Lamb à la Manchèga (p. 64)
Bredee (p. 65)
Porc à la Fermière (p. 69)
Pot Roast Venison (p. 75)
Curried Chicken (p. 81)
Pigeons with Mushrooms or Peppers, Cooked in Sherry (p. 82)
Ratatouille (p. 108)

The Recipes

Soup

Creamy Soups made from Left-overs · Soups made from Frozen Sauces

Owners of small freezers who do not feel justified in allocating storage space to home-made soups will always find room for left-overs that would otherwise be wasted. Many of these bits and pieces—no use on their own—would be good in a soup, since anything edible can be incorporated in soup, though when sweet it must be used with discretion.

Freeze unwanted oddments as soon as possible and store them in one polythene bag. The soup can then be made when wanted or when time is available.

Creamy Soups made from Left-overs

Ingredients:

- left-over foods—cut up, mashed or minced as applicable.
- a good knob of fat—preferably from the top of a casserole, otherwise dripping, butter or margarine.
- choice of liquids—stock, milk, water, beer, cider, wine.
- seasoning—powdered nutmeg or mace, or garlic, onion or celery salt can be used, in addition to salt and pepper.
- additional flavouring—a little lemon juice, vinegar, or one of the manufactured sauces.

Heat the fat in a saucepan and cook the left-overs for about 2 minutes. Remove from heat and stir in enough flour to absorb the fat. Return to heat and cook a further few minutes before stirring in enough liquid to make the paste the consistency of fairly thick custard. Replace over heat and stir until the mixture thickens.

Now you decide whether you want a soup with bits and pieces in it. If not, liquidize the concentrated soup or pass it through a moulin-légumes or sieve.

At this stage the soup, or any of it not wanted shortly, should be poured into rectangular containers, chilled and block frozen (p. 16).

To complete concentrated soup, either freshly made or frozen Place over heat and when hot add any of the chosen liquids to make a soup of the required thickness, also seasonings and extra fancied flavourings.

Soups made from Frozen Sauces

Most of the sauces given on pp. 161–5 will make good soups and are useful when wanted in a hurry. They just need thawing, heating and diluting to the required thickness and quantity with any of the liquids listed on p. 48.
If one sauce fails to make enough soup, two or more can be blended to give interesting results and additional bulk. Cheese Foundation (p. 86) is also a good addition; it provides extra body as well as a pleasant cheesy flavour.

Fish

Fish Cooked in Sauce · Fish Cooked in Rich White Sauce · Fish Soubise · Fish in Onion and Tomato Sauce · Fish Moly · Fish Hollandaise · Fish Mayonnaise · Fish Cakes · Fish Pie · Kedgeree · Baked Cod à la Norge

While still frozen, raw fish can be quickly boiled, steamed, baked, grilled or fried; though if it is to be coated with egg and crumbs or batter, it should first be partially thawed. Therefore it is sensible to freeze it in its raw state, as most people agree that fish is best served as soon as cooked. Exceptions are: recipes made with cooked fish, such as Fish Cakes (p. 51) and Kedgeree (p. 52) and complicated fish dishes, like Baked Cod à la Norge (p. 53).
The following simple recipe can be made with frozen or unfrozen raw fish and a choice of frozen or freshly made sauces. The result is delicious.

Fish Cooked in Sauce

When any fish, from coley to turbot, is cooked extremely slowly in sauce, the fish juices mingle with the sauce and retain their maximum flavour. The sauce must be thick and not allowed to simmer, far less to boil. This means that the oven must be no hotter than 190°–200° F—88°–93° C—Mark 'S' or Low. With fish from the fishmonger or out of the freezer and a selection of frozen sauces, a variety of these excellent dishes can be made with very little trouble. Just put the chosen sauce—about 4 tablespoons (60 ml) to ½ lb (200 g) fish—on the bottom of an oven dish with the fish on top or at the side of the sauce. In the case of fillets, the skin should be uppermost or alternatively flat fish can be rolled. Season to taste, slip the dish into a paper bag and place it in the ultra cool oven. The fish should be cooked in 1–2 hours, depending on the thickness of the fish, whether frozen or not, and the heat of the oven.

To serve Remove any lurking bones, also skin from coarse fish fillets. Place fish on hot serving dish. Stir fish juices into the sauce and check flavour and heat. If sauce was frozen, it may need additional heating. Either pour hot sauce over the fish or serve separately.

The following are examples of Fish Cooked in Sauce

Fish Cooked in Rich White Sauce

Use Basic Rich White Sauce (p. 161).
A choice of the following may be added:

Before or during cooking Chopped parsley or fennel (fresh or dried); anchovy sauce; shrimps; capers; prawns

After cooking Chopped hard-boiled eggs

Fish Soubise

Use Sauce Soubise (p. 163).

Fish in Onion and Tomato Sauce

Use Onion and Tomato Sauce (p. 164).

Fish Moly

Use Moly Sauce (p. 165).

Fish Hollandaise

Use Dutch Sauce (p. 168) and be careful the oven heat does not rise above 190° F–88° C.

Fish Mayonnaise

Use Canadian Mayonnaise (p. 168).
Shrimps or prawns (fresh, tinned or frozen) can be added. Serve cold with salad.

Fish Cakes

These are excellent and could not be easier to prepare. They are made from Fish Cooked in Rich White Sauce (p. 161), plain Mashed Potatoes (p. 117) and dried breadcrumbs. Only about half the quantity of sauce is needed. (If the full quota is used, additional potato is necessary, which will give you more fish cakes but they won't be nearly as good.)
When the fish is cooked, blend it into the sauce with a fork. Add enough potato to make the mixture just manageable, but not stiff. Put the crumbs into a small round basin. Drop heaped tablespoons of the fish mixture, one at a time, into the crumbs. Shake the basin carefully so that the fish cakes bounce round and round, thus becoming circular and crumb covered. Flatten cakes slightly and place them on a plate and store in the fridge until cold and firm.

To serve immediately Fry a golden brown in a deep frying pan with plenty of hot lard.

To freeze Open freeze unfried fish cakes until firm, then pack in polythene bags.

To serve from freezer Fry fish cakes over very gentle heat until they begin to thaw, then raise the heat and brown on both sides.

Fish Pie

Fish Cooked in Rich White Sauce (p. 161) is also the base for Fish Pie. Cook the fish and sauce in a suitable pie dish—a rectangular foil one—if the pie is to be frozen.
Lift the cooked fish on to a plate, remove any skin and bones and flake it before returning to the well-stirred sauce. Top the mixture with Creamed Potato (p. 117).

To serve shortly The dish can either be browned in the oven or under the grill or cooled and stored in the fridge to be reheated and browned as required.

To freeze Chill the un-browned pie, underwrap in clinging film, pack in a polythene bag, seal and freeze.

To serve from freezer Thaw, reheat and brown by placing in a cold oven and cooking at 400° F—200° C—Mark 6 for about 45 minutes or until brown.

Kedgeree

Oven setting 250° F—130° C—Mark ½

In this unorthodox recipe the fish is cooked with the rice. The result is excellent.

Allow per portion (large):

3–4 oz (75–100 g) smoked haddock, without skin or bones
1 dessertspoon (10 ml) vegetable oil
1½ oz (37·5 g) long-grained rice, unwashed
½ small onion, finely chopped (optional)
4 fluid oz (100 ml) boiling water
chopped hard-boiled egg
parsley

Cut the fish into small pieces. Heat the oil in a stew pan or a flame-proof casserole with a well-fitting lid.
Fry the rice and onion, stirring continuously with a wooden spoon until the rice becomes a pale brown. Add the haddock and the boil-

ing water, fasten the lid and, while still boiling, place the pan in the pre-heated oven. Cook 65 minutes.

To serve immediately Add chopped newly hard-boiled eggs and parsley. Serve very hot.

To freeze Put kedgeree into suitably sized rectangular containers. Chill and block freeze (p. 16).

To serve from freezer Put the frozen kedgeree, with a little butter, into a heavy pan over gentle heat to thaw and reheat. When nearly hot enough, add chopped hard-boiled egg and parsley.

Baked Cod à la Norge *Oven setting 425° F—220° C—Mark 7*

This includes vegetables and bread as well as fish, and thus provides a delicious complete light meal.

For 4 portions allow:

1 lb (400 g) cod fillet
4 oz (100 g) butter
6 oz (150 g) carrot, grated
3 oz (75 g) celery, diced
1 medium-sized onion, chopped
4 slices crustless bread, diced
3 tablespoons (45 ml) chopped parsley
seasoning to taste
3 heaped tablespoons (60 ml) soft breadcrumbs

Wash and dry the fish. Remove the skin. Melt three-quarters of the butter and lift the pan from the heat. Add the vegetables, diced bread, parsley and seasoning to the melted butter.

Place fish in pie dish or dishes—rectangular foil ones when fish is to be frozen. Cover with the vegetable bread mixture. Sprinkle with the crumbs and dot with the remaining butter.

To serve immediately Place dish in preheated oven and bake 20–30 minutes.

To freeze Pack the chilled (unbaked) fish in polythene bags, seal and freeze.

To serve from freezer Place frozen fish in a cold oven, set as given. Bake for 30 to 40 minutes.

Meat and Poultry

Simmered Beef and Vegetables · Flemish Braised Steak · Smothered Steak · Boeuf Bourgignonne · Hungarian Goulash · Beef Gobbets · Minute Steaks · Mince Minute Steaks and Onion · Chilli-con-Carne · Hamburgers · Swedish Meat Balls · Lamb à la Manchèga · Bredee · Hungarian Lamb · Likky Frizzle · Breast of Lamb Cutlets · Porc à la Fermière · Chinese Sliced Pork · Barbecued Spare Rib · Veal with Mushrooms and Cream Sauce · Fricassée of Veal · Wiener Schnitzel · Pot Roast Venison · Fried Liver · Liver Cakes · Lambs' Kidneys à la Señorita · Chicken and Rice · Fried Chicken à l'Espagnol · Chicken Marengo · Curried Chicken · Pigeons with Mushrooms or Peppers, Cooked in Sherry

All types of meat and poultry can be successfully frozen.
The recipes given are just a few that have proved especially suitable for small freezers. Economy has also been considered—not only by including dishes that use cheaper cuts, but also those that save fuel, by being cooked on the hob and not in the oven.
After cooking, remove meat and poultry bones before freezing. This saves space.

Simmered Beef and Vegetables

To serve 4 allow:

1 lb (400 g) stewing beef, cut into small pieces
1 oz (25 g) dripping or lard
1 onion, sliced
1 carrot, sliced
1 small turnip, sliced
1 clove garlic, crushed in salt (optional, see p. 24)
pinch of sugar
2 tablespoons flour

salt and pepper to taste
about ½ pint (250 ml) water or stock
a bouquet garni
2 or 3 tomatoes, fresh or tinned, thickly sliced
½ head of celery, cut into 2 in (5 cm) pieces
3 or 4 potatoes, thickly sliced
1 tablespoon (15 ml) chopped parsley

Fry the meat in a frying pan. When slightly brown remove it from the fat and place it in a stew pan with a close-fitting lid.
Put the onion, carrot, turnip and garlic into the frying pan. Sprinkle with sugar. Cover pan, and cook over gentle heat for a few minutes, before lifting the vegetables from the fat and adding them to the meat in the stew pan.
Mix the flour with the remaining fat, cook until brown, then stir in the liquid. Season to taste. Pour the sauce over the meat and vegetables and add the bouquet garni. Fasten the pan lid. After bringing the mixture to the boil, reduce heat to the minimum and allow the meat to simmer extremely gently for 1½ hours. Then remove the bouquet garni and add the remaining vegetables and the parsley. Baste these with the gravy. Bring to the boil and simmer very gently for a further ½–1 hour until the meat is tender.

To freeze Pour the stew into suitable rectangular containers. Chill before block freezing (p. 16).

To serve from freezer Thaw and heat either in a heavy pan over gentle heat or in a heat-proof serving dish in a moderate oven (p. 35).

Flemish Braised Steak *Oven setting 275° F—140° C—Mark 1 or Slow Cooking Method (pp. 44–6)*

Allow per portion:

a piece of braising steak—5–6 oz (125–150 g)
1 tablespoon (15 ml) vegetable oil, seasoned
1 level dessertspoon (10 ml) flour
1 medium onion, sliced

¼ oz (6·25 g) butter
1 oz (25 g) button mushrooms, washed and dried
¼ clove of garlic, crushed in salt (optional, see p. 24)
1 teaspoon (5 ml) dark moist sugar
salt and pepper to taste
3 tablespoons (45 ml) beer or stout

Marinade the steak for 24 hours in the seasoned oil. Remove meat from oil, dry it on absorbent paper and coat with flour.
Fry onions in the butter until brown. Place them together with the mushrooms on the bottom of an oven dish with a close-fitting lid. Add the oil marinade to the butter in the pan and fry the beef until just brown. Place meat on top of the onions and mushrooms.
Mix sugar, seasoning and garlic (if used) with the beer, pour it into the frying pan and swill out the fat and meat juice over the beef. Cover dish and cook until very tender either in the hotter oven for 2–4 hours or by the Slow Cooking Method.

To freeze Place steak in suitable rectangular containers for block freezing (p. 16), and cover with vegetables and gravy. Chill before freezing.
To serve from freezer Thaw and heat either in a heavy pan over very gentle heat or in a heat-proof serving dish in a medium oven (p. 35).

Smothered Steak *Oven setting 350° F—180° C—Mark 4*

Allow per portion:

4–6 oz (100–150 g) braising steak, 1 in (2·5 cm) thick
1 dessertspoon (10 ml) flour
1 onion, sliced
½ green or red pepper, seeded and sliced (optional)
salt and pepper to taste
a little fat for frying
3–4 tablespoons (45–60 ml) stock, beer or cider

Work flour into both sides of the steak with the edge of a heavy saucer. Preferably using a flame-proof casserole, fry the onion and pepper until brown, then push to one side.

Brown the meat on both sides. Add seasoning and liquid. Bring to the boil, cover casserole and place in preheated oven and cook 1¼–1½ hours.

To freeze Place steak in suitable rectangular containers for block freezing (p. 16), and cover with vegetables and gravy. Chill before initial freezing.

To serve from freezer Thaw and heat either in a heavy pan over very gentle heat or in a heat-proof serving dish in a medium oven (p. 35).

Boeuf Bourgignonne *Oven setting 275° F—140° C—Mark 1 or Slow Cooking Method (pp. 44–6)*

To serve 2 allow:

¾ lb (300 g) blade bone, or buttock steak
1 oz (25 g) dripping
¼ lb (100 g) onion, finely sliced
1 rasher lean bacon, chopped
2 oz (50 g) mushrooms, sliced
pinch moist brown sugar
2 teaspoons (10 ml) flour
4 tablespoons (60 ml) Burgundy
a little stock
salt and pepper to taste
bouquet garni

Cut meat into four pieces. Heat the dripping in a flame-proof casserole or a deep frying pan, and sauté the steak. When lightly and evenly browned, remove meat from fat, replace with onions, bacon, mushrooms and sugar and fry over gentle heat. When these are beginning to brown, return meat, sprinkle with flour, add the Burgundy and just enough stock so that the liquor nearly covers the other ingredients. Season, stir well and add the bouquet garni. When using a frying pan, transfer the mixture to a casserole. Cover and place in centre of oven. Either cook 2½–3 hours or until tender in the hotter oven, or use the Slow Cooking Method. Remove bouquet garni.

To freeze Put the steak into suitable rectangular containers and pour the sauce over it. Chill and block freeze (p. 16).

To serve from freezer Thaw and reheat either in a heavy pan over very gentle heat or in an oven-proof serving dish in a medium oven (p. 35).

Rice, spinach or peas and very young carrots go well with this dish.

Hungarian Goulash *Oven setting 275° F—140° C—Mark 1 or Slow Cooking Method (pp. 44–6)*

For each serving allow:

4 oz (100 g) best stewing steak, cut into small pieces
¼ oz (6·25 g) seasoned flour
½ medium-sized onion, chopped
¼ red or green pepper, seeded and chopped
¼ oz (6·25 g) dripping
2 teaspoons (10 ml) tomato purée
1 teaspoon (5 ml) paprika
2½ fluid oz (62·5 ml) stock
1 oz (25 g) fresh skinned tomatoes or tinned tomatoes, quartered
½ teaspoon (2·5 ml) dried mixed herbs or a bouquet garni

Dip the meat in the seasoned flour. Lightly fry the onion and pepper in the dripping, either in a flame-proof casserole or a frying pan. When the onion is clear, add the meat and fry lightly on all sides. Stir in the tomato purée, the paprika and the rest of the seasoned flour. Add the stock, tomatoes and herbs. Cover casserole or transfer the mixture from the frying pan to an ordinary casserole.
Cook in hotter oven either 2½–3 hours or until the meat is very tender, or use the Slow Cooking Method.

To freeze Put the goulash in suitable rectangular containers. Chill before block freezing (p. 16).

To serve from freezer Thaw and reheat either in a heavy pan over gentle heat or in an oven-proof serving dish in a medium oven (p. 35). Serve with rice.

Beef Gobbets

This dish, in favour at the beginning of the last century, is equally at home in our present-day freezers.

Allow per portion:

5–6 oz (125–150 g) braising beef, cut into small pieces
¼ teaspoon (1·25 ml) grated lemon peel
1 teaspoon (5 ml) grated onion or shallot
1 teaspoon (5 ml) chopped parsley
salt, pepper and nutmeg to taste
¼ oz (6 g) butter
½ teaspoon (2·5 ml) vegetable oil
1 teaspoon (5 ml) flour
a pinch dark, moist sugar
a scant 2½ fluid oz (62·5 ml) stock, or water
1 teaspoon (5 ml) each, port and vinegar
1½ heaped tablespoons (40 ml) fresh breadcrumbs
a generous ¼ oz (6 g) melted butter

Mix together the meat, lemon peel, onion, parsley and seasoning. Heat the butter and oil, fry the meat until just brown, then lift it into a heavy pan with a close-fitting lid.
Stir the flour and sugar into the fat and add the liquids. Stir and cook until the sauce thickens before pouring it over the meat. Cover pan and cook very slowly over gentle heat, stirring occasionally, for about 1–1½ hours, or until the meat is really tender. Just before it is cooked, mix the breadcrumbs with the melted butter.
Place the meat in suitably sized rectangular foil dishes and cover it with the crumb mixture.

To serve immediately Brown the hot gobbets under the grill.

To freeze Chill, then either wrap, seal and freeze gobbets in foil containers or block freeze (p. 16) and return meat to containers before thawing.

To serve from freezer Place frozen gobbets in a cold oven, set 375° F—190° C—Mark 5, and cook 30–40 minutes until hot, crisp and brown.

Minute Steaks

You can't compare these with thick juicy steaks, but they are excellent in their own right and ideal when you want to produce a good meal quickly from a small freezer.

Buy fillet steak. It's better to slice it yourself just before freezing. Cut slices ¼–½ in (½–1 cm) thick and allow 1–2 per person. Place slices on a working surface, sprinkle each side with a little salt, preferably sea salt, and bang the steaks with the bottom of a milk bottle to make them larger but thinner. Brush with olive oil.

To freeze Wrap steaks individually in clinging film. Stack them on top of each other and slip them into a polythene bag. Seal and freeze.

To serve from freezer Place frozen steaks in a frying pan with a small knob of butter over very gentle heat. When the steaks begin to thaw, remove the pan and raise heat. Replace the pan over a high temperature and cook the steaks one minute on each side.

Lift steaks on to a hot serving dish. Add a little boiling water and seasoning to the pan and blend well with the butter and meat juices. Pour this over the steaks or serve separately in a very small sauce boat.

Mince Minute Steaks and Onion

These budget versions of minute steaks are really good when not compared too much with their namesakes. They occupy little freezer space and are so quick both to prepare and serve.

For 4–5 steaks allow:

1 lb (400 g) best minced beef
salt and pepper to taste
a little olive oil
½ an onion per portion for serving

Mince the beef twice more and add the seasoning. Shape into flat cakes about 6 in (15 cm) in diameter. Brush both sides with oil and wrap each steak in clinging film. Place one on top of the other on a freezer tray (p. 19).

To freeze Place in the freezer to harden. Then pack in a polythene bag, seal and return to freezer.

To serve from freezer First fry finely sliced onion in a little butter and a teaspoon of olive oil. When a golden brown, lift pan from heat and put onion on a hot serving dish to keep warm. Place the steaks in the hot pan and when they begin to thaw, return pan to heat, adding if necessary a little extra butter. Fry steaks about a minute on each side. Arrange them on the dish with the onions. Pour a little boiling water into the pan, stir it into the fat and meat juices and pour over the steaks.

Chilli-con-Carne

To serve 4 allow:

1 oz (25 g) butter or 1½ tablespoons (25 ml) oil for frying
1 onion, chopped
1 clove garlic, crushed in salt (optional, see p. 24).
1 lb (400 g) minced beef
8 oz (200 g) tin tomatoes
2 tablespoons (30 ml) tomato purée
½ teaspoon (2·5 ml) chilli powder
salt and pepper to taste
8 oz (200 g) tin baked beans

Cook the onion and garlic in a saucepan over gentle heat until the onion is transparent. Add the mince and stir until the meat changes colour. Add the tomatoes, tomato purée and chilli powder. Break up the tomatoes. Stir well, season and bring to the boil. Cover pan and simmer very gently for 30–40 minutes.

To freeze Pour the mixture into suitable rectangular containers, chill and block freeze (p. 16).

To serve from freezer Place frozen block in a pan over gentle heat and add baked beans—an 8 oz (200 g) tin is needed when all the meat mixture is used. Stir occasionally until very hot. Serve with creamed potatoes or boiled rice.

Hamburgers *Slow Cooking Method (pp. 44–6)*

It is worth finding space for these hamburgers in an oven filled with slowly cooked dishes.

For 2 hamburgers allow:

1 slice crustless bread 4 × 2½ × ½ in (10 × 6 × 1 cm)
2 fluid oz (50 ml) boiling stock, or boiling water and ¼ beef stock cube
½ lb (200 g) best minced beef
1 small onion, grated
1 dessertspoon (10 ml) chopped parsley
salt and pepper to taste
1 small egg
browned breadcrumbs
1 tablespoon (15 ml) tomato ketchup
a little water

Place the bread on a large plate. When stock is not available, crumble the stock cube into a measure and add the boiling water. Pour this or the boiling stock over the bread, and mash with a fork. Add the meat, onion, parsley and seasoning. Mix well. Beat the egg and blend it into the mixture. Divide this into two portions. Cut 2 pieces of foil about 8 × 10 in (20 × 25 cm), and sprinkle crumbs on to the centre of each piece. Place the hamburgers on top of the crumbs, sprinkle well with more crumbs and wrap them in the foil. Before the parcels are cooked, place them over a small tin, resting on a grid or on poaching rings.

When the hamburgers have had their spell in the ultra-slow oven, lift them carefully from the foil either into suitable rectangular containers or, *if to be served immediately*, on to a hot serving dish and keep warm.

Now make the sauce by scraping the meat and egg juices from the foil into the tin and adding the tomato ketchup and a little water. Place tin over gentle heat and stir until the mixture is well blended. Pour sauce over the hamburgers.

To freeze Chill before block freezing (p. 16).

To serve from freezer Place frozen hamburgers and sauce in a frying pan over gentle heat. Cover pan with a lid or a plate. When the sauce begins to thaw, stir occasionally and at the same time turn the hamburgers.

Swedish Meat Balls

The fact that these delicious meat balls are so quickly thawed and ready for serving makes them excellent stand-bys and well worth the rather tedious mincing process.

For 6 portions allow:

8 fluid oz (200 ml) milk
1 egg
8 heaped tablespoons (160 ml) fresh breadcrumbs
¼ lb (100 g) best pie veal
2 oz (50 g) lean pork
½ lb (200 g) best minced beef
2 tablespoons (30 ml) finely minced onion
a little butter
salt, pepper and nutmeg to taste

Beat the egg into the milk, add the crumbs and leave to soak. Cut the veal and pork into small pieces and put through the mincer. Mix with the minced beef and mince the lot twice more.
Fry the onion in butter until a golden brown. Mix the meat, the soaked crumbs, onion and seasoning until well blended. Form the mixture into little balls.

To serve immediately Brown the meat balls in a little butter over medium heat then add a little boiling water and proceed as for serving from freezer, p. 64.

To freeze Open freeze on polystyrene trays (p. 19) until meat balls are firm. Then pack, seal and stack.

To serve from freezer Place required meat balls with a knob of butter in a suitably sized frying pan over gentle heat. As they begin to thaw, raise heat and when brown add boiling water to a depth of about an inch (2–5 cm). Cover pan, reduce heat and simmer for 15 minutes.

Lamb à la Manchèga *Oven setting 325° F—170° C—Mark 3 or Slow Cooking Method (pp. 44–6)*

Almost any cut of lamb can be used for this Spanish dish—leg, shoulder, best end of neck, loin. These should be boned and, where applicable, rolled. For about 2 lb (800 g) lamb (boned), allow:

a large knob of butter
a bay leaf
salt and pepper to taste
¼ pint (125 ml) white wine, or dry cider
a green or red pepper, seeded and sliced
a clove of garlic, crushed in salt (optional, see p. 24)
2 tablespoons (30 ml) chopped parsley
a little extra butter

Brown the meat in butter. Put it in a casserole with a closely fitting lid and only just large enough to hold the meat. Add the bay leaf, seasoning and liquid. Cover and cook in the slow or ultra-slow oven until tender.
Shortly before the meat is cooked, fry the pepper, garlic and parsley in a little butter. Pour the sauce from the casserole over these, after removing the bay leaf. Stir well and cook for a few minutes. Carve the meat into slices.

To serve immediately Place slices on a hot dish and pour sauce etc. over the meat.

To freeze Place slices of meat and pepper in suitable rectangular containers, cover with sauce, chill and block freeze (p. 16).

To serve from freezer Thaw and reheat either in a heavy pan over gentle heat or in an oven-proof serving dish in a medium oven (p. 35).

Bredee *Oven setting 275° F—140° C—Mark 1 or Slow Cooking Method (pp. 44–6)*

A tasty, slow-cooked dish from South Africa.

To serve 4 allow:

2 lb (800 g) lean middle neck of lamb
1 oz (25 g) butter, or dripping
1 large onion, sliced
a 15 oz (375 g) tin of tomatoes
¼ teaspoon (1·25 ml) chilli sauce
½ teaspoon (2·5 ml) salt
¼ teaspoon (1·25 ml) pepper, freshly ground
1 teaspoon sugar (5 ml)

Cut meat into pieces. Heat fat in a flame-proof casserole or a frying pan and fry the onion until it begins to brown. Add the meat and fry quickly, stirring continuously. When the meat is brown on all sides, add the other ingredients and, still stirring, cook for a further 2 minutes. If using a frying pan, transfer the mixture to a casserole. Cover and place in the oven. Either use the Slow Cooking Method or cook 2½ to 3 hours or till tender in the hotter oven.
Cut the meat off the bone.

To serve immediately Reheat meat in sauce and place on a hot serving dish.

To freeze Place meat and sauce in suitable rectangular containers, chill and block freeze (p. 16).

To serve from freezer Thaw and reheat either in a heavy pan over gentle heat or in a heat-proof serving dish in a medium oven (p. 35). Serve with Boiled or Fried Rice (pp. 104–5).

Hungarian Lamb

To serve 4 allow:

1½ lb (600 g) lean lamb from leg or shoulder, cut into cubes
1½ oz (37·5 g) butter
1 teaspoon (5 ml) vegetable oil
1 onion, chopped
2 teaspoons (10 ml) paprika
1 tablespoon (15 ml) flour
3 fluid oz (75 ml) white wine
1 tablespoon (15 ml) tomato purée
a bouquet garni
¼ pint (125 ml) chicken stock
salt to taste
¼ teaspoon (1·25 ml) sugar (optional)
¼ lb (100 g) mushrooms, cleaned and sliced
a little extra butter

For serving allow for each portion:

2 tablespoons (30 ml) sour cream (p. 173)
1 teaspoon (5 ml) chopped parsley

Heat the fats in a saucepan and brown the meat. Add onion, paprika, flour and mix well. Stir in the wine and simmer for 5 minutes. Add the tomato purée, bouquet garni, stock, salt and sugar. Cover pan and simmer very gently for 30 minutes. Stir occasionally to prevent sticking.
Gently cook the mushrooms in a little butter.
Remove meat and boil sauce until it is reduced by about a quarter.

To serve immediately Place proportionate amounts of meat, mushrooms and sauce in another saucepan and simmer very gently for about 20 minutes or until the meat is tender. Add the cream and just bring to the boil. Before serving, sprinkle with parsley.

To freeze Return meat to reduced sauce and add the mushrooms. When cold, remove the bouquet garni and spoon the mixture into suitable rectangular containers. Block freeze (p. 16).

To serve from freezer Thaw frozen block in a heavy pan over gentle heat and simmer for about 20 minutes. Add cream and parsley as given for immediate serving.

Likky Frizzle *Oven setting 400°–425° F—200°–220° C—Mark 6–7*

This is an old Devon recipe—it's good, also economical and simple. As for quantities, it's do as you please.

Ingredients required:

lean breast of lamb
potatoes, boiled or steamed and mashed
leeks, boiled and chopped
seasoning to taste

Simmer lamb extremely gently in salted water for about 1½ hours or until the bones can be removed. Lightly score the skin.

To serve immediately Line the bottom and sides of a deep pie dish or baking tin with mashed potato. Put a layer of leeks on top of the potato and cover this with the boned, scored lamb. Cook in preheated oven until brown and crisp. In the meantime, if liked, you can make a little gravy from the stock in which the lamb was simmered.

To freeze Line the bottom and sides of one or more foil pie dishes with mashed potato. Continue as given for serving immediately, but chill the Likky Frizzle instead of cooking it. The same applies to any gravy. Cover the cold dishes with a clinging film, place them in polythene bags, seal and freeze. Pour the gravy into small rectangular containers and block freeze (p. 16).

To serve from freezer Put the Likky Frizzle into a cold oven, set as above, and cook until brown and crisp, about 45 minutes. Thaw and heat the gravy in a small saucepan.

Breast of Lamb Cutlets

Ingredients:

a breast of lamb, as lean as possible
1 onion stuck with 2 or 3 cloves
a bouquet garni
seasoned stock
1 egg, beaten
fresh breadcrumbs
a little flour

Put the meat, onion and bouquet garni in a pan and just cover it with the stock. Simmer very gently for 1½ hours. Remove bones, unwanted fat and skin from meat. Place the breast on a plate or dish, covered with a similar plate or dish with weights on it. Chill the stock after taking out the onion and bouquet garni.
When the meat is cold, cut it into cutlets. Coat these first with egg and then with crumbs. Press the crumbs well into the egg and repeat the process.
Make a gravy, using the stock thickened with a roux made with a little flour and some of the congealed fat.

To serve immediately Fry the cutlets in lard until a golden brown. Serve with gravy and mint sauce or mint jelly; or the cutlets can be served cold.

To freeze Open freeze the freshly crumbed cutlets, before packing them in polythene bags. Seal and return them to the freezer. Pour the gravy into suitable rectangular containers, chill and block freeze (p. 16).

To serve from freezer As given for immediate serving.

Porc à la Fermière *Oven setting 275° F—140° C—Mark 1 or Slow Cooking Method (pp. 44–6)*

To serve 4 allow:

1–1¼ lb (400–500 g) lean pork, cut into 4 portions
1 pig's kidney, sliced
1 dessertspoon (10 ml) seasoned flour
½ oz (12·5 g) butter
1 teaspoon (5 ml) oil
1 onion, sliced
1 stick celery, cut into 1 in (2·5 cm) pieces
3 young carrots, sliced
½ a green or red pepper, sliced; or 2 tomatoes, skinned and sliced
2 oz (50 g) mushrooms, sliced
1 dessert apple, peeled, cored and sliced
1 teaspoon (5 ml) tomato purée
½ chicken stock cube
4 tablespoons (60 ml) white wine, or still cider
bouquet garni

Coat pork and kidney slices in seasoned flour. Heat butter and oil in a frying pan and fry them. When brown, remove meat on to a plate. Reduce heat and place onion, celery and carrots in the pan, adding if necessary a little extra butter. Cover pan and cook slowly until the onion is clear. Lift pan and add the pepper or tomatoes, mushrooms, apple, tomato purée and crumbled stock cube. Mix well with any meat juices in the pan. Put ⅓ of the mixture on the bottom of a casserole. Lay half the meat on top. Repeat these layers and cover the meat with the remaining mixed vegetables. Finally pour in the liquid and bouquet garni, cover the casserole and cook for 3–4 hours or until tender in the hotter oven or use the Slow Cooking Method.

To freeze Put the meat, covered with the vegetables and sauce, in suitable rectangular containers. Chill and block freeze (p. 16).

To serve from freezer To thaw and heat, place frozen block either in a heavy pan over gentle heat or in an oven-proof serving dish in a medium oven (p. 35).

Chinese Sliced Pork

Stage I

To serve 4 allow:

1 lb (400 g) pork fillet from leg, or tenderloin
1 tablespoon (15 ml) cornflour
1 teaspoon (5 ml) sugar—dark moist, if available
1 tablespoon (15 ml) sherry
1½ tablespoons (22·5 ml) soy sauce
2 tablespoons (30 ml) vegetable oil
2 tablespoons (30 ml) hot water

Cut the meat, as wafer thin as possible, into little slices about 1 in (2·5 cm) square. Dredge these on a plate, with the cornflour and sugar. Stir in the sherry and soy sauce.
Heat the oil in a large heavy pan. Add the meat mixture and the hot water. Stir continuously with two wooden spoons for 2 minutes or until the meat is a light brown.

To freeze Place convenient amounts in rectangular containers, chill and block freeze (p. 16).

To serve from freezer Shortly before serving, boil rice or noodles.

Stage II

Assemble per portion of frozen meat mixture:

¼ lb (100 g) frozen string beans or peas (to make meat go further, extra vegetables can be used)
1 teaspoon (5 ml) vegetable oil
1 teaspoon (5 ml) soy sauce
salt to taste

Place the frozen meat mixture into a heavy, adequately sized pan and the chosen frozen vegetable into a saucepan. Place both utensils over gentle heat and add the oil to the vegetables and the soy sauce to the meat. Stir both until the meat has thawed and any vegetable liquid has evaporated. Add the vegetables to the meat and season with salt. Raise the heat and stir until the pork is very hot. Cook for a further minute.
Serve immediately with rice or noodles.

Barbecued Spare Rib *Oven setting 350° F—180° C—Mark 4*

To serve 4 allow:

1–1¼ lb (400–500 g) spare rib (without bones), cut into 4 fairly thick slices
1 medium onion, chopped
½ oz (12·5 g) butter
1 stick celery, chopped
2 level tablespoons (30 ml) moist brown sugar
2 level teaspoons (10 ml) dry mustard
½ teaspoon (2·5 ml) salt
½ level teaspoon (2·5 ml) paprika pepper
2 teaspoons (10 ml) tomato purée
1 tablespoon (15 ml) soy sauce
¼ pint (125 ml) water
1 tablespoon (15 ml) vinegar
2 tablespoons (30 ml) lemon juice, fresh or bottled

Fit the meat slices into a shallow casserole and place in the preheated oven. Cook, uncovered, for 30 minutes or until well browned.
In the meantime, fry the onion until brown. Remove pan from heat and stir in the remaining ingredients. When the meat is browned, pour off any fat. Reheat the mixture in the pan and pour it over the pork. Cover casserole and return to oven, now reduced to 300° F—150° C—Mark 2. Cook for a further hour.

To freeze Place meat in suitable rectangular containers and pour the sauce over it. Chill and block freeze (p. 16).

To serve from freezer Thaw and heat either in a wide shallow pan over very gentle heat or in a serving dish in a moderate oven (p. 35).

Veal with Mushrooms and Cream Sauce

This is an excellent party dish from France. It is cooked very slowly on the hob.

To serve 4 allow:

1–1¼ lb (400–500 g) frying veal, cut into 4 portions
a good knob of butter
1 teaspoon (5 ml) olive oil
salt and pepper to taste
5 fluid oz (125 ml) white wine
¼ lb (100 g) button mushrooms, sliced vertically
about ¼ pint (125 ml) single cream

Fit the veal closely into the bottom of a flame-proof serving dish or shallow, heavy stew pan. Add the butter and oil and cook over very low heat for about 20 minutes or until the veal is tender. During this process add seasoning and, if necessary, a little extra butter.
When the meat is nearly cooked, add the white wine and mushrooms, and when they, as well as the meat, are tender add the cream. Continue to cook gently until the liquid is reduced and the sauce thickened.

To freeze Place the veal in suitable rectangular containers and pour the mushroom sauce over it. Chill and block freeze (p. 16).

To serve from freezer Place block in a flame-proof serving dish or a shallow stew pan over very gentle heat. Stir with a wooden spoon until the sauce has thawed, then stir occasionally (at the same time spooning the sauce over the meat) until hot. Serve with slices of lemon.

Fricassée of Veal

Another veal dish, suitable for guests and cooked on the hob.

To serve 4 allow:

1 lb (400 g) best pie veal, cut into neat pieces
1 medium-sized onion, sliced
a bouquet garni
salt and pepper to taste
1 lb (400 g) young carrots, scraped and sliced
¼ lb (100 g) frozen peas
1 oz (25 g) flour
½ pint (250 ml) milk
1 oz (25 g) butter or margarine

Place the meat, onion and bouquet garni in a large saucepan with a close-fitting lid. Add seasoning and just enough water to cover. Bring to the boil, remove any scum, put on the lid and simmer gently for 1 hour.
Add the carrots and make sure there is sufficient water, if necessary adding a little more. Replace the lid and simmer steadily for a further 20 minutes.
Remove the bouqet garni, check the flavouring and add the frozen peas. Simmer very gently for a further 15 minutes.
Blend the flour with a little of the milk, and stir this into the pan. Add the remaining milk and the butter. Bring to the boil and cook for about 5 minutes, stirring frequently.

To freeze Pour the fricassée into suitable rectangular containers. Chill and block freeze (p. 16).

To serve from freezer Thaw and reheat either in a heavy pan over gentle heat or in a heat-proof serving dish in a medium oven (p. 35).

Wiener Schnitzel

These are ideal standbys for hostesses with small freezers—they take up little space and can be served so quickly.

Schnitzel are made from thin slices or escalopes, cut from leg or fillet of veal, and should be about 5 × 3 in (13 × 8 cm).

Stage I

To serve 4 allow:

4 escalopes (about 1 lb (400 g) meat)
seasoned flour
1 egg, beaten with seasoning and a few drops of oil
about 2 oz (50 g) fresh white breadcrumbs

Trim the escalopes, snip the edges with scissors, and bang them out flat with a cutlet bat or the bottom of a milk bottle. Dip the veal in seasoned flour, and shake before brushing with the egg mixture and completely covering with crumbs. Place the schnitzel between pieces of grease-proof paper and press in crumbs.

To freeze Stack the schnitzel one on top of the other, separated by pieces of waxed paper. Slip into a polythene bag, seal and freeze.

To serve from freezer

Stage II

Allow:

a good knob of butter
1 teaspoon (5 ml) olive oil
to garnish: slices of lemon, capers, pickled gherkins
lemon juice
parsley

Just thaw the frozen schnitzel in a large greased frying pan over very low heat. Remove these from the pan and heat the butter and olive oil over low to moderate heat. Fry the schnitzel for about 7–10 minutes—they should be a rich golden brown—turn only once. Place on a hot serving dish and garnish each one with a slice of lemon, covered with ½ teaspoon (2·5 ml) capers and a slice of pickled gherkin. Stir a squeeze of lemon juice into the butter in the pan and pour over the dish. Sprinkle with a little chopped parsley and serve immediately.

Pot Roast Venison *Oven setting 275° F—140° C—Mark 1 or Slow Cooking Method (pp. 44–6)*

Moderately priced venison, cut in small pieces, is often sold at supermarkets, and is just right for this tasty dish.
Before it is cooked, the venison must be marinaded for at least 2 days.

To serve 4 allow:

1 lb (400 g) cut-up venison

The marinade needs:

4 fluid oz (100 ml) claret
4 fluid oz (100 ml) cold water
½ teaspoon (2·5 ml) salt
4 peppercorns, 6 cloves and 1 bayleaf
1 small onion, finely chopped

Also allow:

about 1 tablespoon (15 ml) flour
2 tablespoons (30 ml) fat
½ teaspoon (2·5 ml) grated lemon peel
1½ tablespoons (22·5 ml) lemon juice
1½ tablespoons (22·5 ml) port
½ teaspoon (2·5 ml) sugar
seasoning to taste

Make the marinade in a covered dish and soak the meat, turning it occasionally.
After 2 days or longer, remove meat, drain and dredge it with flour. Heat fat in a frying pan and fry the meat until brown, then place it in a casserole. Add enough flour to the fat remaining in the pan to make a roux. Cook this for a minute. Add the marinade and the rest of the ingredients. Stir well and continue cooking until the

sauce thickens. Strain the sauce over the meat, mix and cook either in a preheated oven for $2\frac{1}{2}$–3 hours or until tender, or use the Slow Cooking Method.

To freeze Spoon the venison and sauce into suitable rectangular containers. Chill and block freeze (p. 16).

To serve from freezer Thaw and reheat either in a heavy pan over very gentle heat or in a heat-proof serving dish in a medium oven (p. 35).

Fried Liver

Lambs', pigs' or calves' liver can be prepared and frozen as follows. Buy the liver in one piece. Just before freezing, cut it into slices, as thin as possible. Dip these first in seasoned, beaten egg, then in brown breadcrumbs.

To freeze Lay the slices in layers on a polystyrene tray (p. 19) dividing the layers with waxed paper. Wrap the lot in clinging film, slip it into a polythene bag, seal and freeze.

To serve from freezer Place slices of liver in a greased frying pan over very gentle heat. Remove them from pan as soon as they are thawed. Raise heat and put in the pan lard or dripping for frying. When hot, replace the liver and cook it as short a time as possible. It is done once no blood exudes when slices are punctured and when they are brown on both sides.
Fried liver is good served with any of the following: Onion and Tomato Sauce (p. 164), Bacon Potato Cakes (p. 89), Grilled Sausages (p. 93).

Liver Cakes

To serve 4 allow:

2 oz (50 g) bacon, cut into pieces
2 oz (50 g) margarine, or butter
1 medium onion, finely chopped
12 oz (300 g) any liver, sliced

¼ lb (100 g) mushrooms, sliced
2 tablespoons (30 ml) chopped chives, or spring onions
1 tablespoon (15 ml) chopped parsley
1 egg, beaten
fresh breadcrumbs
lard or dripping for frying

Put the bacon in a frying pan over slow heat until it exudes plenty of fat. Add 1 oz (25 g) of the margarine or butter, raise the heat, add the onion and cook until it is transparent. Remove bacon and onion from pan and set aside. Place the remaining ounce of fat in the pan and cook the liver until just brown. Remove and set aside with the bacon and onion. Fry the mushrooms, adding more margarine or butter if necessary.

Finely mince the liver, bacon and onion. Stir into the mixture the mushrooms, herbs and seasoning. Form into cakes. Dip these first in beaten egg and then in fresh breadcrumbs. Put lard or dripping in a clean pan and fry the cakes a golden brown. Drain on absorbent kitchen paper.

To freeze Chill cakes before packing them in polythene bags, sealing and freezing.

To serve from freezer Place frozen Liver Cakes on a baking sheet in a cold oven, set 400° F—200° C—Mark 6, and cook about 30 minutes or until hot. If liked, sauce can be served with the cakes—Onion and Tomato (p. 164), Mustard Cream Sauce (p. 162), Sauce Soubise (p. 163), Sauce Espagnol (p. 169) are all suitable.

Lambs' Kidneys à la Señorita

A delicious, popular dish from Madrid, suitable for party suppers.

To serve 4 allow:

12 button mushrooms
about ½ oz. (12·5 g) butter and ½ teaspoon (2·5 ml) olive oil
5 or 6 lambs' kidneys, cut into very thin slices
salt and pepper to taste
a small onion, finely chopped

1 dessertspoon (10 ml) chopped parsley
4 or 5 tablespoons (60 or 75 ml) white wine
about ¼ pint (125 ml) Sauce Espagnol (p. 169)
½ lb (200 g) frozen peas
garnish (if liked): quartered hard-boiled eggs and strips of fried gammon

Heat the butter and oil in a deep frying pan, lightly cook the mushrooms, then lift them on to a plate and set aside. Put the kidneys in the pan with the fat and mushroom juices. Add seasoning, onion, parsley and wine. Cook fairly quickly for 3–4 minutes—no longer. Add Sauce Espagnol, frozen peas and the cooked mushrooms. Bring to simmering point and cook gently for a few minutes till the kidneys and peas are cooked.

To freeze Spoon the mixture into suitable rectangular containers. Chill and block freeze (p. 16).

To serve from freezer Thaw and reheat frozen block in a thick frying pan over low heat. As soon as possible, break up block with a wooden spoon, then stir gently until the kidneys are very hot. Place on a hot serving dish with chosen vegetables and, if liked, garnished with quartered hard-boiled eggs and strips of fried gammon.

Chicken and Rice *Oven setting 250° F—130° C—Mark ½*

To serve 4–5 allow:

1 oz (25 g) butter
about 2 lb (800 g) chicken joints
¼ lb (100 g) lean bacon rashers, cut up
tinned tomatoes, strained from a small tin
1 tablespoon (15 ml) olive oil
3 medium or 2 large onions, chopped
3½ oz (87·5 g) long-grained rice, unwashed
8 fluid oz (200 ml) boiling liquid, made up with liquid from tin of tomatoes and water and ½ chicken stock cube
seasoning to taste

Heat the butter in a pan and fry the chicken until brown all over. When nearly brown add the bacon. Cut up the tomatoes and stir them into the bacon and butter. Cook for a further 2 minutes. Lift pan from heat.
Pour the oil into a flame-proof casserole or a stew pan with a well-fitting lid. Place over medium heat and when hot, add the onions and rice. Cook until the onion is transparent and the rice a pale brown, stirring continuously. Add the chicken, bacon and tomatoes and pour in the boiling liquid. Season to taste. When boiling again, fasten lid on pan and place in preheated oven. Cook for 65 minutes.
Remove bones and skin from chicken and divide flesh into portions.

To freeze Place portions of chicken and rice into suitable rectangular containers. Chill and block freeze (p. 16).

To serve from freezer Thaw and reheat frozen blocks in a heavy pan over very gentle heat. Stir rice frequently to prevent sticking.

Fried Chicken à l'Espagnol

This good, practical dish adds taste to broiler birds and cooking costs are minimal. Unless your butcher will dismember poultry, it is easier to buy joints.

To serve 4 allow:

4 chicken joints, weighing about 2 lb (800 g)
3 tablespoons (45 ml) flour
1 teaspoon (5 ml) salt
½ teaspoon (2·5 ml) freshly ground pepper
6 oz (150 g) lard
2 medium-sized onions, sliced
1 green or red pepper, seeded and sliced
4 sticks celery, cut into 1 in (2·5 cm) lengths
4–5 tomatoes (fresh) skinned and sliced, or (tinned) cut into quarters
1 teaspoon (5 ml) salt and a dash of cayenne.

Flatten the joints as much as possible. Put flour and seasoning into a paper bag. Add the joints one by one and shake until well dredged. Heat the fat in a large deep frying pan and when moderately hot, after shaking off excess flour from the chicken joints, put them in the pan, skin side down. The fat should come halfway up the joints. If it does not, add extra lard. Fry gently (there must be no spluttering or smoking fat) until the undersides are well browned, this should take 15 minutes. Turn the chicken and slowly brown the remaining sides. Lift out the chicken and pour off most of the fat, leaving just enough to fry the vegetables. First fry the onion until clear; then add the pepper and celery and fry another 2 minutes. Lastly stir in the tomatoes and seasoning. Lay the chicken on top of the vegetables. Partly cover the pan, making sure the steam can escape. Lower heat and simmer for 10 minutes or until the chicken is really tender and the meat can be removed from the bones.

To freeze Place the chicken meat in suitable rectangular containers and pour the sauce over it. Chill and block freeze (p. 16).

To serve from freezer Thaw and reheat either in a heavy pan over gentle heat or in an oven-proof serving dish in a moderate oven (p. 35).

Chicken Marengo

This old recipe, said to have been improvised by Napoleon's chef when on active service and short of butter, is just as useful today in our freezers, as a standby for unexpected guests.

To serve 4–6 allow:

about 12 pickling onions; or 2 sliced onions
about 12 button mushrooms
butter for frying
1 chicken, jointed; or equivalent chicken joints
3 tablespoons (45 ml) oil
3 tomatoes, cut up
1 tablespoon (15 ml) tomato purée

a sprinkling of well-seasoned flour
6 tablespoons (90 ml) each, white wine and chicken stock
1 clove garlic, crushed in salt (optional, see p. 24)

Brown the onions and mushrooms in a little butter and set aside. Put the oil in a saucepan and, when hot, add the chicken joints. Cook till a golden brown on all sides. Add the tomatoes and tomato purée. Sprinkle the joints with the seasoned flour and stir until the flour browns. Add the liquid, mushrooms, onions, garlic, and check the seasoning. Lower the heat and simmer very gently for 1–1½ hours or until the chicken is tender. Remove flesh from bones and divide into portions.

To freeze Place in suitable rectangular containers. Chill and block freeze (p. 16).

To serve from freezer Thaw and reheat frozen blocks either in a heavy pan over very gentle heat or in an oven-proof serving dish in a medium oven (p. 35).

Curried Chicken *Oven setting 275° F—140° C—Mark 1 or Slow Cooking Method (pp. 44–6)*

When there is a block of Curry Sauce (p. 165) in the freezer, nothing could be easier to prepare than Curried Chicken. If this sauce is not available, it can quickly be made—some of it used for the curry dish and the balance frozen for future use.

To serve 2–3 allow:

about 1 lb (400 g) chicken joints*
about 6 tablespoons (90 ml) Curry Sauce

Place the chicken and sauce in a casserole, cover and either cook for about 2½ hours or until tender in the hotter oven, or use the Slow Cooking Method.
When cooked, remove bones and skin from chicken, divide the

* Any meat that can be casseroled can be used in this recipe in lieu of chicken.

flesh into neat pieces and return to sauce. Should this sauce be too thick, dilute it with chicken stock, milk or water.

To serve immediately Shortly before the chicken is cooked, boil the rice (p. 104) and prepare some of those delicious little odds and ends —salty, sweet and piquant—called sambals. These add the finishing touch to a good curry and are served on little dishes or saucers. Choose a selection from these suggested sambals:

salted nuts
chopped anchovies
chopped stuffed olives
potato crisps
chopped cucumber
chopped tomato
chopped peppers
Bombay duck (a tinned dried fish, must be fried)
mango chutney
cocktail onions
chopped mixed pickles
sliced banana
pineapple pieces
peeled grapes
lychees
diced apple with lemon
diced beetroot
chopped preserved or crystallized ginger
dried fruit
sliced gherkins
chopped pickled walnuts

To freeze Spoon chicken and sauce into suitable rectangular containers, chill and block freeze (p. 16).

To serve from freezer Thaw and reheat frozen blocks in a heavy pan over very gentle heat. During this process prepare the necessary amount of boiled rice and a selection of the sambals given above.

Pigeons with Mushrooms or Peppers, Cooked in Sherry

Oven setting 275° F—140° C—Mark 1 or Slow Cooking Method (pp. 44–6)

Pigeons are usually available and not expensive. Many people find one bird sufficient for two, but others can easily manage one apiece. Pigeons can be deceptive, look plump and tender but prove extremely tough. Therefore it's safer to cook them slowly in a casserole. The following recipe is good and never fails.

For 2 pigeons allow:

olive oil
a little flour
salt and pepper
4 thin rashers streaky bacon
1 onion, grated
1 stick celery, cut up (optional)
1 medium carrot, sliced
¼ lb (100 g) mushrooms, sliced; or 1 medium pepper, seeded and sliced
2½ fluid oz (62·5 ml) sherry
2½ fluid oz (62·5 ml) water
½ oz (12·5 g) butter

Brush the pigeons lavishly with the oil, dredge with flour and season well with salt and pepper. Cover the breasts with bacon, and place the birds with the vegetables in a casserole with a tightly fitting lid. Add the liquid and butter in small dabs. Cover and cook either in the hotter oven for 2½–3 hours or until the birds are tender, or use the Slow Cooking Method.

To serve immediately Place the pigeons—either whole or cut in halves—on a hot, deep serving dish with the vegetables.

To freeze Cut the breast off the birds in two neat pieces, and as much as you can get off the legs, etc. Place this in suitable rectangular containers, cover with the vegetables and sauce, chill and block freeze (p. 16).

To serve from freezer Thaw and reheat frozen blocks either in a heavy pan over gentle heat or in an oven-proof serving dish in a medium oven (p. 35).

Light, Savoury and First Course Dishes

Eggs Soubise · Curried Eggs · Celery à l'Italien and Eggs · Savoury Omelettes · Cheese Aigrettes · Cheese Foundation · Welsh Rarebit · Buck

Rarebit · Celery Rarebit · Cheese Pancakes · Cheese Omelette · Cheese Foundation Sauce · Cheese Eggs · Croque Monsieur · Cheese Foundation in Sandwiches · Cheese Foundation in Soup · Bacon Potato Cakes · Cheese Bacon Potato Cakes · Bacon and Onion Roll · Quiche Lorraine · Miniature Quiches Lorraine · Grilled Sausages · Sausage Pinwheels · Sausage Rolls · Cornish Pasties and Curry Puffs · Pancakes · Miniature Pancakes · Cheese Pancakes · Rice Soufflés: Kidney, Liver and Bacon, or Chicken Liver · Kidney or Liver Pilaff · Spaghetti Bolognese · Lasagne · Pizza · Mushroom Filling · Fillings from Left-over Casseroles · Haddock Filling · Lambs' Kidney Filling · Liver and Bacon Filling · Chicken Liver Filling · Store-cupboard Fillings · Boiled Rice · Fried Rice

Eggs Soubise

Newly poached eggs or eggs en cocotte
hot Sauce Soubise (p. 163)
hot Onion Rings (p. 116)

Place the eggs on a hot serving dish or individual dishes. Pour the hot sauce over them and surround with Onion Rings.

Curried Eggs

Freshly cooked hard-boiled eggs
hot Curry or Moly Sauce (p. 165)
hot rice, Boiled or Fried (pp. 104–5)
any sambals from p. 82 (optional)

Cut the eggs into halves. Place them on a hot dish, surrounded by the rice. Pour the sauce over the eggs. The sambals can be served separately or mixed with the eggs and sauce.

Celery à l'Italien and Eggs (p. 111)

Savoury Omelettes

Omelettes are always favoured as quickly prepared light meals—and when a choice of frozen savoury fillings is available, these can be made much more substantial.

For each omelette allow:

- 2 large eggs
- 1 dessertspoon water
- salt and pepper to taste
- $\frac{1}{2}$ oz (12 g) butter
- about 6–8 teaspoons hot savoury filling (pp. 101–4); or Cheese Foundation (p. 86)

Beat eggs and water lightly together, then season. Heat the butter in a 7 in (18 cm) non-stick frying pan, or special omelette pan, until sizzling but not brown. Pour in the beaten eggs. As these begin to set, move the edges towards the centre with a fork, and at the same time tilt the pan quickly in all directions so that the uncooked egg flows to the edges. Drop teaspoons of the chosen hot filling or Cheese Foundation over the setting omelette. The underneath should be lightly browned and the top still slightly moist. Fold omelette in half, while still in the pan, slide it on to a hot plate and serve immediately.

Cheese Aigrettes

These are useful to have on tap—just right for cheese and wine parties or to serve with aperitifs, as a starter with salad, or hot, as an accompaniment to savoury dishes.

Ingredients:

- 2 oz (50 g) butter
- $\frac{1}{4}$ pint (125 ml) water
- 2 oz (50 g) plain flour
- 2 eggs, beaten
- 2 oz (50 g) grated cheese, including a little parmesan
- $\frac{1}{4}$ teaspoon (1·25 ml) each, salt and dry mustard
- a pinch of cayenne
- oil for frying

Melt the butter in a saucepan. Add the water and bring to the boil. Add flour and beat vigorously with a wooden spoon until the

mixture forms a ball and leaves the sides of the pan clean. Remove from heat. Cool slightly before gradually adding and beating in the eggs. Lastly beat in the cheese and seasoning.
Drop teaspoonsful of the mixture into hot oil and deep fry until a golden brown. Drain on absorbent paper. Serve hot or cold (but still very crisp).

To freeze Chill and open freeze before packing in polythene bags, sealing and freezing again.

To serve from freezer Put frozen cheese aigrettes in a cold oven and bake for about 15 minutes at 400° F—200° C—Mark 6.

CHEESE FOUNDATION AND SOME WAYS OF USING IT

Cheese Foundation

With a supply of Cheese Foundation, you can quickly produce varied cheese dishes or a good strong cheese sauce.

Allow:

1 egg
1 dessertspoon (10 ml) dry mustard
1 teaspoon (5 ml) Worcester sauce
6 fluid oz (150 ml) beer, or milk
½ lb (200 g) grated cheese
½ oz (12·5 g) butter, or margarine

Break the egg into a medium-sized saucepan. Stir into it the mustard, sauce, liquid and cheese. Add the fat. Place pan over medium heat and stir until the mixture thickens.
Cheese Foundation can be stored for a month in a fridge and for up to 6 months in a freezer.

To freeze Pour the foundation into suitable rectangular containers. Chill and mark into sections before block freezing (p. 16).

Welsh Rarebit

For each serving allow:

1 piece toast
2–3 tablespoons (40–50 ml) Cheese Foundation

Either spread Foundation on toast, making sure the crusts are covered, or lay slices of block-frozen Foundation on the toast. Heat and brown under the grill or in the oven. As soon as the frozen cheese begins to thaw, spread it over the toast.

Buck Rarebit

This is a Welsh Rarebit served with a poached egg on top.

Celery Rarebit

To serve 2 allow:

1 or 2 sticks of celery
2 slices toast
6 tablespoons (90 ml) Cheese Foundation
a little finely grated cheese.

Cut celery into neat pieces. Boil in a little salted water until just soft. Heat the Cheese Foundation in a pan over gentle heat. Mix in the celery, and pour the mixture over the toast. Top with the grated cheese. Brown under a hot grill.

Cheese Pancakes

For each pancake (pp. 97–8) allow:

1 tablespoon (15 ml) Cheese Foundation
1 teaspoon (5 ml) grated parmesan; or 1 dessertspoon (10 ml) grated Cheddar cheese

Heat both the pancakes and Cheese Foundation. Spread hot pancakes with hot Cheese Foundation. Roll them up. Place them in a grill pan. Sprinkle with cheese and brown under the grill. Serve immediately.

Cheese Omelette see Savoury Omelettes (p. 84)

Cheese Foundation Sauce (p. 163)

Cheese Eggs

To serve 2 allow:

- 3 hard-boiled eggs
- 5 tablespoons (75 ml) Cheese Foundation
- 1 teaspoon (5 ml) chopped parsley, or dried chervil
- 1 tablespoon (20 ml) milk; or 2 teaspoons (10 ml) each milk and tomato ketchup

Slice the eggs thinly and place in an oven dish. Measure the Cheese Foundation into a small pan and place over gentle heat. Add the liquid and blend well. When hot, add the parsley or chervil and pour the sauce over the eggs. Either put the dish in preheated oven, 450° F—230° C—mark 8, or under a hot grill until sizzling hot and brown on top.

Croque Monsieur

Ham is intended for this useful French recipe, but tins of corned beef or luncheon meat are also good.

For each serving allow:

- 2 slices of bread, crusts removed
- 2–3 tablespoons (30–45 ml) Cheese Foundation, thawed if frozen
- 1 or 2 thick slices cooked ham; corned beef; or luncheon meat
- a little French mustard (optional)
- lard or dripping (if fried)
- a little parsley (optional)

Spread one side of each piece of bread with the Cheese Foundation and make a sandwich with the meat and mustard as the filling. Fry in plenty of hot lard or dripping or toast each side under the grill. Either garnish with fried parsley and serve immediately, or the Croque Monsieur can be chilled, wrapped in film, packed in a polythene bag and frozen.

To serve from freezer Either thaw and heat in a medium oven or under a low grill and garnish with fried parsley.

Cheese Foundation in Sandwiches

Thawed Cheese Foundation is excellent in tomato and cucumber sandwiches.

Cheese Foundation in Soup (p. 49)

Bacon Potato Cakes

These are good and useful to serve with eggs, sausages, liver, with cheese as a savoury, or instead of potatoes with any suitable dish. Use bacon pieces or rashers of streaky bacon. The former are the better buy; being on the fatty side is an advantage and they are so much cheaper.

Weigh bacon after removing rinds and allow:

the same weight boiled potatoes
quarter that weight self-raising flour
pepper to taste
a little chopped onion fried in butter (optional)
a little chopped parsley (optional)
1 egg for about ½ lb (200 g) bacon

Cut bacon into small pieces and place in the top of a double saucepan or a basin that fits over a saucepan. Cook covered, over boiling water for 35–40 minutes.
Mash or finely grate the potatoes.

When the bacon is cooked and has exuded plenty of fat, remove from heat and beat in the other ingredients.
Drop heaped tablespoons of the mixture either into a frying pan containing hot fat or on to a well-greased baking sheet. Flatten the heaps into round cakes about ½ in (1 cm) thick. Either fry the cakes, brown them on both sides and drain on absorbent paper or bake in preheated oven, 400° F—200° C—Mark 6, for 20 minutes or until nicely brown.

To freeze pack the chilled cakes in layers on a polystyrene tray (p. 19), the layers separated by waxed paper. Slip the lot into a polythene bag. Seal and freeze.

To serve from freezer Reheat either in a lightly greased pan over very low heat or in a fairly hot oven for 15 to 20 minutes or under a very low grill. Serve hot.

Cheese Bacon Potato Cakes

Place frozen Bacon Potato Cakes (p. 89) under a very low grill. When they begin to thaw, cover them with finely grated cheese, raise the heat and grill until the cheese has melted and is beginning to brown. Serve hot.

Bacon and Onion Roll

This is another nice adaptable dish that can be made with inexpensive bacon pieces.

For about 8 slices allow:

8 oz (200 g) bacon pieces, or streaky, or flank rashers
1 oz (25 g) butter, or margarine
4 oz (100 g) onion, chopped
4 oz (100 g) self-raising flour
2 tablespoons (30 ml) semolina
6 heaped tablespoons (120 ml) fresh breadcrumbs
¼ pint (125 ml) shredded beef suet
1 dessertspoon (10 ml) chopped parsley
1 egg beaten with a very little water

After removing rind, cut the bacon into small pieces and place in the top of a double saucepan or a basin that fits over a saucepan. Cook over boiling water for 20 minutes.
In the meantime, melt the butter in a small pan and cook the onion gently until clear. Place the flour, semolina, crumbs, suet and parsley in a fairly large basin and mix them together.
When the bacon is cooked, lift it and the onion with a fork or perforated spoon on to a plate and mix them together.
Make a well in the flour mixture and drop in the beaten egg. With a fork, work the surrounding flour into the egg, adding the liquor and butter from the bacon and onion pans, also if necessary a little water to make a pliable dough. Place this on a floured working surface and roll it into a rectangle about ⅛ in (¼ cm) thick, 9 in (23 cm) wide and as long as you can get it. Spread the dough with the bacon and onion. Roll it up as firmly as possible and tie it up in a cloth or cooking film. Boil for ½ hour.
Cut off any slices wanted for immediate serving and quickly cool the rest of the roll.

To freeze Cut the cold roll into slices and pack in polythene bags with film or waxed paper between slices.

To serve from freezer

Method 1. Completely wrap slices in foil and heat in boiling water. Serve hot slices with or without a sauce; Onion and Tomato Sauce, Sauce Soubise, or any of the sauces given on pp 162–7 are suitable.

Method 2. Heat the slices in boiling water as above, cover them with grated cheese and brown under the grill.

Method 3. Place the frozen slices in a shallow oven-proof serving dish. Cover them with slices of frozen sauce, place in a cold oven, set 375° F—190° C—Mark 5, and bake about 20 minutes. After the first 8 minutes, spread the thawed sauce well over the slices.

Quiche Lorraine *Oven setting 375° F—190° C—Mark 5*

To serve 4–5 allow:

6 oz (150 g) General Purpose Shortcrust Pastry Dough (p. 152)
1 egg and 1 egg yolk
1 oz (25 g) grated cheese
seasoning to taste
¼ pint (125 ml) single cream (milk can be used)
½ oz (12·5 g) butter
2 oz (50 g) bacon, diced
1 small onion, finely sliced; or 12 spring onions

Place a 7 or 8 in (18 or 20 cm) flan ring on a greased baking sheet, or use a loose-bottomed flan tin. Line it with the pastry dough. Place bread crusts or greaseproof paper and beans on the bottom and bake blind in a preheated oven for 10 to 15 minutes.
Beat the eggs in a basin before adding the cheese, seasoning and cream. Melt the butter in a small pan and add the bacon, onion or spring onions (left whole) and cook slowly until soft but not brown. Then tip the contents of the pan into the mixture in the basin and mix well. Pour this filling into the par-baked pastry case. Raise oven to 425° F—220° C—Mark 7. Bake the quiche at that temperature for 5 minutes, then reduce to 350° F—180° C—Mark 4 for about 30 minutes or until firm and a golden brown. Serve hot or cold.

To freeze Chill rapidly. If the quiche is wanted in the near future and freezer space allows, pack it uncut in a polythene bag; otherwise cut into wedges, wrap these in clinging film and pack in bags alternating wedge tips and bases. Seal and freeze.

To serve from freezer If to be served hot, place in a moderate oven for about 20 minutes; if to be served cold, thaw overnight in the fridge.

Miniature Quiches Lorraine *Oven setting 400° F—200° C—Mark 6*

For these the above mixture is cooked in baked Tartlet Cases (p. 157). The filled cases are cooked for 5 minutes in the hot oven and then a further 10–15 minutes, the oven reduced to 350° F—180° C—Mark 4.

To serve from freezer Thaw and reheat 5–10 minutes in a fairly hot oven.

Grilled Sausages

It's a good idea to keep a few grilled sausages in the freezer. These can provide a meal on their own or make a useful addition to other dishes.

To freeze Chill freshly grilled sausages. Wrap them separately, in pairs or in threes in clinging film, pack in a polythene bag, seal and freeze.

To use from freezer Thaw and heat either under a very low grill, in a heavy pan over very gentle heat, or together with the frozen dish with which they are to be served.

Sausage Pinwheels *Oven setting 400° F—200° C—Mark 6*

For 12 Pinwheels allow:

10 oz (250 g) General Purpose Short Crust Dough (p. 152)
8 oz (200 g) sausage meat
1 tablespoon (15 ml) tomato purée
1 teaspoon (5 ml) made mustard (optional)
salt and pepper to taste
beaten egg

Roll the dough into an oblong about $\frac{1}{8}$ in ($\frac{1}{4}$ cm) thick.
Blend together the sausage meat, purée, mustard and seasoning and

spread the mixture on the dough to within 1 in (2·5 cm) of the edges. Brush the edges with a little beaten egg or water. Roll up along the long side and seal. Cut into 12 slices. Place these on a greased baking sheet and flatten them with your hands or a palette knife. Brush with beaten egg and bake in a preheated oven 20–25 minutes. Serve hot or cold.

To freeze Chill before packing in polythene bags, sealing and freezing.

To serve from freezer Whether to be served hot or cold, pinwheels are crisper when thawed and heated in a moderate oven or under a slow grill.

Sausage Rolls *Oven setting 475° F—240° C—Mark 9*
or 400° F—200° C—Mark 6

It is always useful to have sausage rolls in the freezer—a few substantial ones for a quick meal or a picnic—tiny ones to serve with drinks. They are made with:

sausagemeat or sausages (not skinless but skins removed)
Puff Pastry Dough (p. 153); or Shortcrust (p. 152) (the former is preferable)

The procedure is as follows:

1. With well-floured hands, roll the sausagemeat, or the skinned sausages placed end to end, into long sausages.
2. Roll the dough into a rectangle. Puff pastry should be thin—⅛ in (¼ cm) at most, shortcrust may be thicker.
3. Lay an elongated sausage, equal in length to the width of the pastry, on the front of the dough. Leave about ½ in (1 cm) uncovered dough in front of the sausage.
4. Brush sausage with cold water.
5. Turn front edge of dough over the sausage.
6. Roll dough away from yourself until the sausage is covered with dough.

7. Cut the dough about ½ in (1 cm) away from the roll.
8. Brush edge with cold water, and complete the rolling operation.
9. Cut the long sausage roll into suitable lengths.

Repeat stages 3 to 9 until all the sausage is used.

For immediate use Place sausage rolls on a cold baking sheet in a preheated oven—the higher temperature for puff pastry. Bake about 15 minutes.

To freeze Pack chilled uncooked sausage rolls in sealed polythene bags.

To use from freezer Shortly before serving or packing or on the day of the party, place the frozen sausage rolls in a cold oven, set as given, and bake about 20–25 minutes.

Cornish Pasties and Curry Puffs

Both are good ways of using joint and vegetable left-overs. They freeze well unbaked, and can be stored for up to a month.

Cornish Pasties are good made with General Purpose Shortcrust Pastry Dough (p. 152) or Rough Puff (p. 156) or Puff Pastry Dough, but Curry Puffs are best made with Puff Pastry (p. 153).

To make pasties and curry puffs Cut off a piece of dough for each pasty or puff—you will soon discover how much dough you need for the size of pasty required. Roll these pieces into approximate squares; don't worry about making them over-symmetrical or cut the edges, but roll puff dough thin, ⅛ in (¼ cm) at most; rough puff and short doughs may be a little thicker. Put the filling on to the front half of each square, leaving about ½ in (1 cm) of dough round the front and sides. Fold these dough edges over the filling. Brush them with a little water. Fold the uncovered dough over the filling on to the moistened edges. Press gently into position.

To freeze Wrap the uncooked pasties or puffs in clinging film, pack them in polythene bags, seal and freeze.

To use from freezer Cut two ventilation slits in the dough and, if a glaze is wanted, brush with beaten egg, egg and milk, or just milk.

Place on a baking sheet in a cold oven, set according to the type of dough. Bake until pastry is cooked.

The fillings These must be partly improvised according to the foods at your disposal, but the following give some indication, and are intended to fill 2 large or 4 small pasties or puffs.

Cornish Pasty Filling

$\frac{1}{4}$–$\frac{1}{2}$ oz (6·25–12·5 g) butter, or margarine, or dripping
1 small onion, shredded
2 teaspoons (10 ml) flour
1–2 fluid oz (25–50 ml) left-over gravy, or stock
salt and pepper to taste
1 medium-sized cooked potato
about 2 oz (50 g) cooked meat
1 cooked swede (or 3 cooked brussels sprouts, or a few runner or broad beans, or any other cooked vegetables)
Worcester sauce to taste

Melt the fat in a saucepan and cook the onion until clear. Add flour, stir with a wooden spoon and cook for 2 minutes, stirring all the time. Remove pan from heat, and gradually mix in the liquid. Cook again, still stirring, until the sauce thickens. Add seasonings. If the meat is really tender, cut into cubes, otherwise mince it. Add meat and cut-up potato and vegetables to the sauce. Mix well and chill before making the pasties.

Curry Puff Filling

$\frac{1}{2}$ oz. (12·5 g) butter, or margarine
1 small onion, finely sliced
1 small cooking apple, peeled, cored and sliced
$\frac{1}{2}$ clove garlic, crushed in salt (optional, see p. 24)
1 dessertspoon (10 ml) flour
$\frac{1}{2}$–1 dessertspoon (5–10 ml) curry powder; or $\frac{1}{2}$–1 teaspoon (2·5–5 ml) curry paste

¼ teaspoon (1·25 ml) salt
1 teaspoon (5 ml) black treacle, or marmalade
1 teaspoon (5 ml) chutney
3 fluid oz (75 ml) milk

Melt the fat in a saucepan and cook the onion for about 2 minutes. Add the apple and garlic. Cover pan and cook over a gentle heat until the apple is mushy. Remove from heat, and stir in the flour, curry powder or paste and salt. Cook for a minute, stirring with a wooden spoon. Add the remaining ingredients, and cook the mixture again until it thickens.

To this base add available cooked meat (cut in small cubes, minced or shredded) together with any of the following:

salted nuts
mixed pickles, chopped
dried fruit
oranges, cut in small pieces
grapes, peeled and pipped
pineapple, cut in small pieces
green and red peppers (fresh or tinned) cut in thin slices

Chill the mixture before making the curry puffs.

Pancakes

Attractive meals, starters and sweets can be produced in next to no time when a freezer contains pancakes and quickly heated fillings for them.

To make 7–9 pancakes allow:

2 oz (50 g) plain flour
¼ teaspoon (1·25 ml) salt
1 whole egg and 1 egg yolk
1 tablespoon (15 ml) oil, or melted butter
¼ pint (125 ml) liquid—equal parts milk and water
a little butter for greasing pan

Sieve the flour and salt into a small mixing bowl. Make a well in the centre and drop in the egg, the extra yolk and the oil or melted butter. Gradually stir the flour into the egg and oil and, at the same

time, slowly pour in the liquid. When all the ingredients are well blended, beat the batter vigorously with a wire spoon, a whisk or a fork. Cover and leave to stand in a cool place for at least an hour.
Beat the batter again and transfer to a jug.
Heat a 7 in (18 cm) heavy frying pan (an omelette pan is ideal) and melt a small knob of butter, about the size of the top of your thumb. When sizzling, pour in a little batter and tip the pan this way and that to give it a thin even coating of batter. Cook over good heat until the pancake begins to brown, loosen round the edge with a palette or pliable knife, toss or turn the pancake over and cook the other side.
Cool pancakes on a tea towel.

To freeze and serve from freezer See following recipe.

Miniature Pancakes

These are excellent for starters or to serve with drinks. They are made with the above batter, which should yield about 40 little pancakes.
Pour the mixture from a dessertspoon on to the hot buttered pan and, using the bottom of the spoon, spread into as thin and symmetrical rounds as possible. Cook as given for the larger pancakes.

To freeze When quite cold, pile full-size pancakes one on top of the other, separated by pieces of waxed paper and arrange miniature pancakes in layers on sheets of cooking film (e.g. 'Look'). Slip both types into polythene bags (if liked, made rigid, p. 19), seal and freeze.

To serve from freezer Place frozen pancakes (miniatures still on cooking film) on an enamel plate, over a large saucepan of boiling water. Make sure the pancakes do not overlap the sides of the saucepan. Cover the plate. Fill hot pancakes with savoury (pp. 101–4) or sweet (p. 125) fillings and roll them up.

Cheese Pancakes are made with Cheese Foundation (p. 87)

Rice Soufflés: Kidney, Liver and Bacon, or Chicken Liver *Oven setting 375° F—190° C—Mark 5*

Made with Kidney Filling (p. 102), Liver and Bacon Filling (p. 103), or Chicken Liver Filling (p. 104).

For each serving allow:

about 2 oz (50 g) filling
about 3 heaped tablespoons (60 ml) Boiled Rice (p. 104)
1 teaspoon (5 ml) olive, or sunflower oil
1 egg yolk, beaten
salt and pepper to taste
1 egg white, whisked

If frozen, the filling must be thawed before it is thoroughly blended with the rice, oil and egg yolk. Season and fold the egg white into the mixture.
Spoon into a greased soufflé dish and bake in preheated oven 15–17 minutes.

Kidney or Liver Pilaff

Made with Kidney Filling (p. 102), Liver and Bacon Filling (p. 103), or Chicken Liver Filling (p. 104).

To serve 2 allow:

2 servings hot Fried Rice (p. 105).
about ¼ lb (100 g) hot filling

Stir the hot filling into the hot rice and serve immediately.

Spaghetti Bolognese

For each serving allow:

about 2 oz (50 g) spaghetti
a little butter
about 3 tablespoons (45 ml) hot Italian Meat Sauce (p. 170)

a little chopped parsley
a little grated cheese, preferably parmesan

Cook the spaghetti gently in plenty of boiling water for 15 minutes or until tender. Drain well and return to pan. Stir in a knob of butter.
Pile the spaghetti on a hot dish. Spoon over the hot sauce, sprinkle with parsley and serve immediately, the grated cheese served separately.

Lasagne *Oven setting 375° F—190 C°—Mark 5*

This is made with lasagne (long broad strips of pasta, sold at most supermarkets), Italian Meat Sauce and a cream sauce, made with Basic Rich White Sauce and cheese. Though the made-up dish would freeze satisfactorily, for reasons of space-saving it is preferable to cook the pasta when required and use sauces from the freezer. The sauces, cheese and pasta are packed in layers into a deep well-greased oven dish. Start with a layer of meat sauce, cover this with cream sauce and a sprinkling of cheese and then a layer of cooked lasagne,* if necessary trimmed to fit, with the ends turned up the sides of the dish. These layers should be repeated, at least once before adding the final layers of meat sauce, cream sauce and cheese. It is a go as you please recipe, but as a rough guide, for 3–4 servings allow:

about half the Italian Meat Sauce recipe (p. 170)
½–¾ pint (250–375 ml) cream sauce, made with Basic Rich White Sauce (p. 161) diluted with milk, top of the milk, or single cream and seasoned with salt, pepper and ground nutmeg
2–3 oz (50–75 g) grated cheese
4–6 oz (100–150 g) lasagne pasta

Throw the pasta strips into a large pan of boiling water. Boil until really tender, 20–30 minutes. The moment it is cooked pour a jug of cold water into the saucepan. Strain immediately and spread on a clean cloth before making the lasagne.

* Oven-ready lasagne pasta is now available.

Bake the prepared lasagne in preheated oven for about 20–30 minutes.

Pizza (p. 180)

SAVOURY FILLINGS

For Pancakes (p. 97), Pastry Cases (p. 157), Vol-au-Vents and Bouchées (p. 158) and Omelettes (p. 84).

All the following fillings can be block frozen (p. 16) and thawed in a heavy pan over gentle heat.

Mushroom Filling

1 oz (25 g) butter
1 teaspoon (5 ml) olive or sunflower oil
½ lb (200 g) mushrooms, sliced
salt, pepper and nutmeg to taste
1 tablespoon (15 ml) grated onion
1 tablespoon (15 ml) chopped parsley
3 or 4 tablespoons (45 or 60 ml) cream or top of the milk

Heat butter and oil in a frying pan over gentle heat and cook the mushrooms for a minute, stirring with a wooden spoon. Add the remaining ingredients. Still stirring gently, continue to cook, but not longer than 4 minutes.

Fillings from Left-over Casseroles

Left-over casseroles, not wanted within a few days, can be frozen to make excellent pancake, vol-au-vent and pastry case fillings, for the coming months.
Strain the solids from the sauce and, if necessary, cut them up. Mix in some sauce—about half as much as the solids. Bring to the boil.

Haddock Filling

For bouchées and miniature pancakes:

8–10 oz (200–250 g) smoked haddock fillet
1 gill (125 ml) milk
1 oz (25 g) butter or margarine
1 oz (25 g) flour
½ teaspoon (2·5 ml) lemon juice, fresh or bottled
2–3 tablespoons (30–45 ml) single cream, or top of milk

Wash haddock, place in a frying pan with the milk and simmer 10 minutes. Remove skin and any bones and flake the fish into little pieces.
Melt fat in a small pan and mix in the flour. Stir and cook for a few minutes without browning. Gradually add the haddock-flavoured milk, stirring continuously. Simmer very gently for 5 minutes. Add and blend the flaked fish, the remaining ingredients and, if necessary, seasoning.
Mark the filling into sections with the back of a knife before block freezing (p. 16).

Lambs' Kidney Filling

This filling can also be used in Kidney or Liver Pilaff (p. 99) or Kidney or Liver Rice Soufflé (p. 99).

4 lambs' kidneys
½ teaspoon (2·5 ml) flour
salt and pepper to taste
2 oz (50 g) butter
either ¼ lb (100 g) sliced mushrooms; or ½–1 red or green pepper, seeded and sliced; or 2 large or 4 small tomatoes, skinned and sliced
1 teaspoon (5 ml) chopped parsley
a few drops of lemon juice, fresh or bottled
½ glass sherry (optional)

Cut the kidneys into halves, and each half into three. Sprinkle these with the flour and seasoning.
Melt the butter in a fairly small pan. When hot, add the kidneys and the prepared chosen vegetable. Stir continuously with a wooden spoon and cook rather quickly for 3 to 4 minutes—no longer or the kidneys will toughen. Add the remaining ingredients, give the final stir and at the same time scrape the bottom of the pan.

Liver and Bacon Filling

This filling is also used in Liver and Bacon Rice Soufflé (p. 99) or Kidney or Liver Pilaff (p. 99). It is made with lambs' or calves' livers.

1 oz (25 g) butter
1 teaspoon (5 ml) olive or sunflower oil
2 rashers streaky bacon, cut into strips
1 small onion, grated
4 oz (100 g) liver, cut into thin 1 in (2·5 cm) strips
1 tablespoon (15 ml) flour
salt and pepper to taste
either ¼ lb (100 g) mushrooms, finely chopped; or 1 red or green pepper, seeded and finely chopped; or 2 large or 4 small tomatoes, skinned and finely chopped
1 tablespoon (15 ml) chopped parsley
a pinch of dried mixed herbs
a little lemon juice, fresh or bottled

Melt the butter and oil in a saucepan over gentle heat and cook the bacon and onion until they are both clear.
In the meantime, shake the liver in a paper bag with the flour and seasoning. When the bacon is cooked, add the liver. Stir it with a wooden spoon and as soon as it changes colour, add the other ingredients. Lower the heat a little and cook for a further 3 minutes, still stirring to prevent sticking.

Chicken Liver Filling

This filling is also used in Chicken Liver Rice Soufflé (p. 99) or Kidney or Liver Pilaff (p. 99).

8 oz (200 g) chicken livers
2 tablespoons (30 ml) flour, seasoned
2 oz (50 g) butter or margarine
2¼ tablespoons (35 ml) sherry

Cut the liver into thin strips and dredge with the seasoned flour. Melt the butter or margarine in a pan over gentle heat and cook the liver until just brown. Lower the heat, add the sherry, cover pan and simmer gently for 5 minutes.

Store-cupboard Fillings

You can face any emergency with tins of:

fish, meat, creamed mushrooms, sweetcorn (cream style), sweet red peppers, tomatoes, any of the condensed soups, together with your own pancakes or pastry cases.

A tin of fish or meat blended with one of the creamed vegetables or mixed with peppers or tomatoes and a little creamed soup, makes a good filling and can be served hot or cold.

Rice

Cooked rice can be frozen, but as it takes only a short time to prepare, it does not seem worth allocating space in small freezers, except for small quantities of surplus cooked rice.

Boiled Rice

There are quite a few methods for boiling rice, and one of the simplest is to pour unwashed long-grained rice into your largest container, nearly filled with fast-boiling salted water. Allow it to boil rapidly, uncovered, for exactly eleven minutes. Then strain it immediately in a large wire or nylon sieve—don't use a colander. The rice can now, if the grains are not quite separate, be held under a hot tap and tossed with a fork. Either serve immediately or place rice in a hot covered container, stir in about 1 tablespoon olive or sunflower oil and keep hot in the oven until served—it will not spoil.

To freeze Rinse in plenty of cold water. Drain well, chill, and freeze in polythene bags.

To use from freezer Either plunge frozen rice into boiling salted water, bring back to the boil and simmer just under a minute before straining; or reheat in a heavy pan with a little olive or sunflower oil or melted butter.

Fried Rice *Oven setting 250° F—130° C—Mark ½*

To serve about 2 allow:

1 tablespoon (15 ml) vegetable oil
3 oz (75 g) long-grained rice (unwashed)
8 fluid oz (200 ml) slightly salted boiling water, or stock

Heat the oil in a stew pan or flame-proof casserole with a very well-fitting lid. Fry the rice, stirring occasionally with a wooden spoon, until it becomes a pale brown. Pour in the boiling liquid. Fasten the lid and, while still boiling, place in the oven. Cook for 65 minutes. The fried rice can be used immediately, or kept hot in the warming-oven.

To freeze Pack chilled rice in polythene bags.

To use from freezer Either thaw rice over gentle heat or in a moderate oven.

Vegetables, Salads and Herbs

Blanching and Freezing Vegetables · Ratatouille · Braised Red Cabbage · Sweet Sour Cabbage · Celery à l'Italien · Celeriac · Celeriac in Sauce · Buttered Celeriac · Celeriac Purée · Celeriac Salad · Buttered Carrots · Buttered Mushrooms · Harvard Beet · Marrow Casserole · Courgette Casserole · Onion Rings · Plain Mashed Potatoes · Potato Croquettes · Duchess Potatoes · Potato Cakes · Sauté Potatoes · Bacon Potato Cakes · Beetroot Salad · Celeriac Salad

Obviously those of us with small freezers cannot freeze vegetables in any quantity; but as most vegetables are frozen commercially, we can always keep a reasonable selection. Yet we should know how to freeze vegetables so that when friends give us garden-fresh produce—often more than we can use at the time—we can preserve the surplus for the months ahead.

THE BLANCHING AND FREEZING OF VEGETABLES

1. Only really fresh vegetables in prime condition will give first class results; so get on with the job as soon as possible.
2. Wash and prepare vegetables as for cooking—except avoid slicing French and runner beans; snap or cut them into 1–1½ in (2–3 cm) pieces. Leave broad beans in their pods until after they have been blanched.
3. The blanching (scalding in boiling water) of vegetables is to slow down the actions of enzymes which eventually cause deterioration; it is applied to vegetables that are usually cooked before eating (marrows are exceptions and are better cooked before freezing).

Blanch at most ½ lb (200 g) vegetables in at least 4 pints (2 litres) water. If more than ½ lb of vegetables is to be frozen, two large saucepans will be needed; failing that, one large saucepan and a large bowl. Drop the vegetables into a saucepan of fast-boiling water. The water must return to the boil within 1 minute of the vegetables' entry. If it doesn't, next time reduce the weight of vegetables or increase the amount of water. *Cover pan and time the blanching from the moment the water has returned to the boil*

VEGETABLE	MINUTES REQUIRED IN BOILING WATER
Asparagus (depending on thickness)	2–4
Artichokes, Jerusalem (according to size)	5–7
Aubergines	4
Beans, Broad (in pods)*	5
Beans, French and Runner (cut into pieces)	2
Broccoli Spears	3
Brussels Sprouts	4
Carrots (sliced or diced)	3
Carrots (whole)	5
Cauliflower (divided into flowerettes)	3
Celery†	3
Corn-on-the-Cob (according to size)	5–8
Courgettes	2
Parsnips (sliced)	2
Peas	2
Spinach	2
Turnips (sliced)	4

4. Strain the blanched vegetables in a large sieve or a colander (over the second saucepan or bowl if more vegetables are to be blanched. Saved blanching water can be used up to six times for the same kind of vegetables).
5. The strained vegetables must be cooled as quickly as possible either in cold water containing ice or in running water, but be careful that a forceful tap does not damage the vegetables.
6. Drain the vegetables and dry them between pieces of absorbent kitchen paper.
7. Pack in polythene bags (p. 20), and freeze.

To serve from freezer See chart, pp. 37–8.

* Shell the beans before cooling.

† Sticks of celery (also the odd tomato, sliced onion and peppers, see pp. 29–30) to be used in recipes may be frozen without blanching.

Commercially Frozen Vegetables

It will be found more economical to buy these in 2 lb (800 g) packs and repack them in small polythene bags.

VEGETABLE DISHES

Contrary to most cooked vegetables, the following vegetable dishes, when they are reheated, lose none of their original quality. This means they are suitable for freezing.

Ratatouille

This vegetable stew from the South of France is not cheap; but the recipe can be varied, according to taste and the state of the purse, by increasing or decreasing the quantity of any of the given vegetables.

To serve 4–5 allow:

- ½ lb (200 g) courgettes, unpeeled and sliced; or marrow, peeled and sliced
- 1 aubergine, unpeeled and sliced
- 3 tablespoons (45 ml) olive oil
- 3 medium onions, sliced
- 2 cloves of garlic, crushed in salt (optional, see p. 24)
- 2 green or red peppers, seeds removed, and sliced
- 2 tomatoes, skinned, seeds removed, and sliced
- ½ teaspoon (2·5 ml) salt
- ¼ teaspoon (1·25 ml) freshly ground pepper

Sprinkle sliced courgettes and aubergine with salt and leave on a plate for 15–20 minutes. Dry them on absorbent paper.
Heat the oil over gentle heat in a flame-proof casserole or a stew pan. Cook the onion and garlic for 2 to 3 minutes. Add the courgettes or marrow, aubergine and peppers. Cook for a further 5 minutes before adding the remaining ingredients. This mixture must

not be fried, but cooked, covered, very slowly until the vegetables are soft and have absorbed the oil. This can be done either over very low heat on the hob for at least 1 hour, or in a preheated oven (300° F—150° C—Mark 2) for about 2 hours, or by the Slow Cooking Method (pp. 44–6).
Ratatouille can be served hot, or cold as an hors d'oeuvres.

To freeze Spoon the mixture into suitable rectangular containers, chill and block freeze (p. 16).

To serve from freezer Either thaw and heat in a heavy pan over gentle heat or in an oven-proof serving dish in a moderate oven. If to be served cold, thaw either overnight in the fridge or about 6 hours at room temperature, or, if wanted in a hurry, see p. 120.

Braised Red Cabbage

This can be served as a hot vegetable or cold, as a salad.

To serve 6 allow:

1½–2 lb (600–800 g) red cabbage, finely shredded
1 onion, sliced
1 oz (25 g) butter
2 cooking apples, peeled, cored and sliced
2–3 tablespoons (30–45 ml) wine vinegar
1 tablespoon (15 ml) sugar
salt and pepper to taste
1 tablespoon (15 ml) soft margarine } creamed together
2 teaspoons (10 ml) flour }

Wash, quarter and remove cabbage stalk before shredding. Put it into a large pan of boiling water and boil for exactly 1 minute. Drain well.
Heat the butter in the same pan, and cook the onion until clear. Add the sliced apple and cook for a further 2–3 minutes. Add the cabbage, vinegar, sugar, seasoning and 2–3 tablespoons water. Mix well. Cover with buttered paper and pan lid. Either cook 40–50 minutes over very gentle heat or for 1½–2 hours in a cool oven (325° F—

170°C —Mark 3). Stir occasionally, adding if necessary a little extra water.
When very tender, add the blended butter and flour, little pieces at a time, to thicken the cabbage juices. Adjust seasoning.

To freeze Place cabbage in suitable rectangular containers, chill and block freeze (p. 16) or chill and pack in polythene bags (p. 20).

To serve hot from freezer Place frozen cabbage in a covered saucepan over gentle heat, stirring occasionally until thawed. Increase heat and cook until very hot.

To serve cold from freezer Thaw in the fridge overnight, at room temperature about 6 hours or, if wanted in a hurry, see p. 120.

Sweet and Sour Cabbage

This is good hot as a vegetable or cold as a salad, which is useful when lettuces become too expensive.

For 1 lb (400 g) finely shredded white cabbage, allow:

¼ pint (125 ml) boiling water
½ teaspoon (2·5 ml) salt
a pinch of bicarbonate of soda
1 large onion, finely chopped
1½ tablespoons (22·5 ml) sunflower or olive oil
1 tablespoon (15 ml) sugar
2 tablespoons (30 ml) vinegar
¼ teaspoon (1·25 ml) ground nutmeg
seasoning to taste

Put the boiling water, salt and soda in a large saucepan. Add the cabbage and onion and boil, covered, for 5 minutes. Add the remaining ingredients. Bring back to boiling point and stir continuously until the moisture has evaporated.

To freeze Spoon the cabbage into suitable rectangular containers and block freeze (p. 16).

To serve from freezer Either thaw and heat in a heavy pan over gentle heat or, if to serve cold, thaw in the fridge overnight, at room temperature about 6 hours or, if wanted in a hurry, see p. 120.

Celery à l'Italien *Oven setting 375° F—190° C—Mark 5*

This, as well as a vegetable, when served with eggs, makes a good light meal.

To serve 2 or 3 allow:

1 large head of celery
boiling water
6 fluid oz (150 ml) milk
2 oz (50 g) butter or margarine
salt and pepper to taste
1 egg, beaten
soft breadcrumbs
a little extra butter

Wash the celery, divide into sticks and cut these into 2 in (5 cm) lengths. Boil for 6 minutes. Strain and return to pan with milk, fat and seasoning. Simmer very gently until tender. Set aside and allow to cool, before stirring in the beaten egg. Butter one or more shallow dishes; if to be frozen use rectangular foil dishes. Sprinkle thickly with crumbs. Pour in the celery and sauce. Cover well with more crumbs and place little pieces of butter on top.

To serve immediately Before serving, bake in preheated oven (365° F—190° C—Mark 5) until the sauce has set and the top is brown. If not wanted immediately, the celery can be stored, uncooked, in the fridge for a few days.

To freeze Chill the unbaked celery and either wrap, seal and freeze in foil container or block freeze (p. 16) and return celery to its container before thawing.

To serve from freezer Place celery in cold oven, set as above, and bake about 30 minutes or until nicely browned.

Celeriac

This celery-flavoured root—obtainable from the end of November to the end of February—can be used as a vegetable to be served with most dishes, or as a salad. It is delicious and freezes well. Before celeriac is used in the given recipes, it must first be prepared as follows:

Peel the roots. Cut into quarters and these into halves. Drop pieces immediately into a pan of salted boiling water and cook until tender, about 15 minutes. Drain and use in one of these recipes:

Celeriac in Sauce

For 1 lb (400 g) boiled celeriac, cut into slices, allow:

1 oz. (25 g) butter, or margarine
1 tablespoon (15 ml) flour
¼ pint (125 ml) water in which celeriac was boiled
¼ pint (125 ml) milk
½ a chicken stock cube
a little lemon juice and sugar (optional)
salt and pepper to taste

Brown the fat and flour in a saucepan. Add the liquid and stock cube and cook until the sauce thickens. Add lemon, sugar and seasoning. Stir in the celeriac and bring the sauce back to the boil.

To freeze Spoon into suitable rectangular containers. Chill and block freeze (p. 16).

To serve from freezer Thaw and reheat either in a heavy pan over gentle heat or in an oven-proof serving dish in a moderate oven (as given for casseroles, p. 35).

Buttered Celeriac

Ingredients:

hot, freshly boiled celeriac (p. 112) cut into strips
butter, sufficient to coat the celeriac
chopped parsley or chives
a little lemon juice (optional)
seasoning to taste

Blend these gently together. *Freezing* and *Serving from freezer* are as given for Celeriac in Sauce.

Celeriac Purée

Either pass hot, freshly boiled celeriac (p. 112) through a moulin-légumes, a sieve, or put it into an electric blender. If liked, plain boiled potatoes (up to ⅓ of the weight of celeriac) can be added before blending. Stir in melted butter (3 oz (45 g) to 1 lb (400 g) purée). Season to taste.

To freeze Spoon the mixture into suitable rectangular containers. Chill and block freeze (p. 16).

To serve from freezer Put the frozen block into a heavy saucepan over gentle heat. Add a little more butter and, if liked, some cream or top milk. Stir frequently until the purée is very hot. Serve garnished with chopped parsley.

Celeriac Salad (p. 121)

Buttered Carrots

These are worth freezing, being useful and versatile. They can be served as a hot vegetable on their own or mixed with peas, as a garnish or in salads and hors-d'oeuvre.
Use young carrots. They must be finely sliced either lengthwise or across. Pour boiling water to a depth of about ½ in (1 cm) into a

pan, just large enough to hold the carrots. Add salt and butter (about 2 oz (50 g) to 1 lb (400 g) carrots). Place over moderate heat and, when boiling, add the carrots. Cover pan and cook until most of the water has evaporated; then with a wooden spoon stir gently until all the water has gone. Check the seasoning. Cool and, if liked, add chopped parsley or chives.

To freeze Spoon the carrots into suitable rectangular containers and block freeze (p. 16).

To serve from freezer Thaw and heat in a heavy pan over low heat or, when wanted cold, place overnight in the fridge or about 6 hours at room temperature. If in a hurry, see Salads on p. 120.

Buttered Mushrooms

This is a satisfactory way of freezing mushrooms. Being cooked, they take up less storage space and once thawed can be used in so many ways. For ½ lb (200 g) mushrooms, sliced, allow about 1 oz (25 g) butter and seasoning to taste.
Heat the butter in a small pan and add the mushrooms and seasoning. Cook gently, stirring occasionally with a wooden spoon, until the mushrooms are cooked. This must not take longer than 3–4 minutes.

To freeze Spoon the mushrooms and the black, buttery liquid into suitable rectangular containers, chill and block freeze (p. 16).

To use from freezer Thaw in a heavy pan over gentle heat.

Harvard Beet

For 1 large or 2 small cooked beetroots, cut into cubes or slices, allow:

2 teaspoons (10 ml) cornflour
2 tablespoons (30 ml) sugar
4 tablespoons (60 ml) each, vinegar and water
2 oz (50 g) butter or margarine
salt to taste

Mix the cornflour and sugar in a pan. Stir in the liquids and add the fat. Place pan over medium heat and stir continuously until the mixture boils. Add the beetroot and, when it begins to boil, reduce heat and simmer gently for 15 minutes. Add salt.

To freeze Spoon the beetroot into suitable rectangular containers, chill and block freeze (p. 16).

To serve from freezer Thaw and heat frozen block in a heavy pan over gentle heat.

Marrow Casserole

Oven setting 275° F—140° C—Mark 1

For 1¼–1½ lb (500–600 g) peeled and seeded marrow, allow:

2 tablespoons (30 ml) seasoned flour
2 oz (50 g) butter
1 onion, sliced (optional)
4 fluid oz (100 ml) milk
salt and pepper to taste

Cut the marrow into cubes and shake them in a bag with the seasoned flour. Melt the butter in a flame-proof casserole or a stew-pan over gentle heat. If onion is used, cook until transparent. Add the marrow and cook for a few minutes before adding the milk. Check seasoning. Bring to the boil, cover and place immediately in preheated oven. Cook 60 minutes—less if marrow is very young.

To freeze Spoon the marrow into suitable rectangular containers, chill and block freeze (p. 16).

To serve from freezer Thaw and reheat either in a heavy pan over gentle heat or in an oven-proof serving dish in a moderate oven (as given for casseroles, p. 35).

Courgette Casserole

Wash the courgettes and slice them, unpeeled, into pieces of about 1 in (2·5 cm). They are then prepared the same way as given for marrows in the previous recipe, except the onion is omitted and the courgettes only need about 45 minutes in the oven.

Onion Rings

These freeze most successfully and make excellent additions to grilled or fried meat, bacon, sausages or eggs. (See Eggs Soubise, p. 84.)

Allow:

$4\frac{1}{2}$ oz (112·5 g) plain flour
$\frac{1}{2}$ teaspoon (2·5 ml) salt
$1\frac{1}{2}$ teaspoons (7·5 ml) cream of tartar
$\frac{3}{4}$ teaspoon (3·75 ml) bicarbonate of soda
1, 2 or 3 onions—according to size
1 egg
1 tablespoon (15 ml) tomato ketchup
1 dessertspoon (10 ml) Worcester sauce
1 tablespoon (15 ml) milk
water (enough to make up the required quantity)
(together amounting to 6 fluid oz (150 ml))
lard for frying

Sieve the flour and dry ingredients into a fairly large pudding basin. Cut the onions into $\frac{1}{8}$ in ($\frac{1}{4}$ cm) slices and using thumbs, push out the individual rings. Break the egg into a measure and beat in the liquids. Gradually add this mixture to the flour, beating continuously with a fork or a wire or perforated spoon. Heat enough lard to fill a pan to a depth of at least 1 in (2·5 cm). Immerse a few onion rings at a time in the batter. Lift each one separately with a fork and drain off surplus batter before placing it in the hot fat. Fry rings on both sides until crisp and a light brown. Place fried rings on a cake tray covered with absorbent paper.

To freeze When cold, pack in polythene bags, seal and freeze.

To serve from freezer Place rings on a cold baking sheet in a cold oven set 375° F—190° C—Mark 5 and cook about 10 minutes.

Plain Mashed Potatoes

These are both simple and extremely useful.
Either boil peeled potatoes or steam or pressure-cook them in their skins.
When cooked, immediately drain the potatoes.
Return peeled boiled potatoes to the dry hot pan and place for a moment over heat to evaporate any moisture.
Steamed or pressure-cooked potatoes need only be peeled.
Mash the cooked potatoes with a fine potato masher, a moulin-légumes or grate them on a fine grater.

To freeze Pack the mashed potato firmly into suitable rectangular containers. Chill and block freeze (p. 16).

To use from freezer When Creamed Potatoes are to be served: Place the frozen block, with a little milk and butter, in a heavy pan over gentle heat. As the milk begins to boil, work it and the melted butter with a fork into the thawing potato. Season with salt and pepper and add extra milk as necessary. Continue to beat the mixture until hot.
When the plain mashed potato is wanted for a recipe, thaw it either overnight in the fridge or for about 4 hours at room temperature.

Potato Croquettes

The time taken for preparing and freezing these potatoes is fully justified when they are so easily and quickly produced for planned or spontaneous parties.

To yield about 8 croquettes allow:

1 lb (400 g) freshly boiled, steamed or pressure-cooked potatoes
½ oz (12·5 g) butter
1 egg yolk
salt and pepper to taste

a little seasoned flour
a beaten egg
browned breadcrumbs
fat for frying

Cook and mash the potatoes as given for Plain Mashed Potatoes (p. 117). Beat in the butter, egg yolk and seasoning.
When sufficiently cool, divide the mixture into small cylinders. Dredge these with seasoned flour, brush with beaten egg and roll them in crumbs. Fry croquettes in deep fat until golden brown. Drain well on absorbent paper, and when cold place on trays, see p. 19.

To freeze Open freeze croquettes and when firm pack in polythene bags, seal and stack.

To serve from freezer Thaw and heat in preheated oven, 400° F—200° C—Mark 6, for about 20 minutes.

Duchess Potatoes

These, like Potato Croquettes, do take some trouble to prepare, but are also splendid for entertaining, when they take no trouble at all.

For 1 lb (400 g) potatoes, freshly boiled, steamed or pressure-cooked, allow:

1–1½ oz (25–37·5 g) butter
1 egg or 2 egg yolks
salt and pepper to taste
a pinch of nutmeg
a little warm milk
beaten egg (optional)

Cook and mash the potatoes as given for Plain Mashed Potatoes (p. 117). Mix in the butter, egg or egg yolks and seasoning. Add just enough warm milk to enable the mixture to be piped. Put it into a forcing bag with a ½ in (1 cm) star pipe. Pipe the mixture on to polystyrene trays (p. 19) and, if liked, brush with a little beaten egg.

To freeze Open freeze the potatoes on their trays until quite firm. Then lift them and pack in polythene bags, seal and return to freezer.

To serve from freezer Place frozen Duchess Potatoes on a greased baking sheet in a preheated oven, 400° F—200° C—Mark 6. Bake until heated through and lightly browned—about 10 minutes.

Potato Cakes

These are as good for everyday use as they are for entertaining.

For 1 lb (400 g) freshly boiled, steamed or pressure-cooked potatoes, allow:

1½ oz (37·5 g) butter or margarine
1 egg yolk, beaten with
1 tablespoon (15 ml) milk
4 level tablespoons (60 ml) self-raising flour
seasoning to taste
1 egg white, stiffly whisked

Cook and mash the potatoes as given for Plain Mashed Potatoes (p 117). Just melt the fat and pour it into a basin with the egg yolk and milk. Gradually stir in the mashed potato, flour and seasoning. Lastly fold in the whisked egg white.

To serve shortly Place heaped tablespoons (20 ml) of the mixture into greased tartlet cases. These can be stored for up to 24 hours in the fridge. Just before serving, bake the potato cakes for about 15 minutes in a hot oven.

To freeze Pack the uncooked mixture firmly into suitable rectangular containers to a depth of about 1½ in (4 cm). Chill and freeze until just frozen but not too solid. Eject the blocks and cut into cubes. Pack these in polythene bags, seal and return to freezer.

To serve from freezer The frozen cubes can either be fried or baked. To fry, place them with a little fat in a frying pan over medium heat. As they begin to thaw, press them into flat round cakes and turn every now and then. Fry until heated through and brown on both sides. To bake, place frozen cubes on a greased baking sheet in a hot oven and continue as given for frying.

Sauté Potatoes

For freezing, these are prepared as usual with firm boiled, steamed or pressure-cooked potatoes, cut into slices. It is specially important that these are fried in clean, odourless fat.

To freeze Drain the freshly fried potato on absorbent paper and leave until cold. Then place on polystyrene trays (p. 19) and open freeze. Pack the frozen potato in polythene bags, seal and return to the freezer.

To serve from freezer Bake frozen potato on a baking sheet in a medium hot oven until hot—about 15 minutes.

Bacon Potato Cakes (p. 89)

SALADS

Since green salads cannot be frozen, if salads are to be stored in the freezer they must be a cooked variety. These cooked salads should be block frozen (p. 16), and are best thawed overnight in the fridge or for about 6 hours at room temperature. However, in an emergency, with a little trouble they can be served within 15 minutes from frozen as follows: Break up the frozen block and place the pieces on the bottom of a shallow dish standing in a larger dish or a baking tin containing boiling water. Rotate the pieces of frozen salad until partly thawed; then remove the smaller dish and allow complete thawing to take its natural course.

Beetroot Salad

Young beetroots are best, preferably newly cooked and still warm. Slice these as thinly as possible and coat well with French Dressing (p. 171). If liked, chopped parsley or chopped chives can be added.

Celeriac Salad

Dice hot freshly boiled (slightly undercooked) celeriac (p. 112). Mix carefully with French Dressing (p. 171) and chill.

To freeze Pack in suitable rectangular containers and block freeze (p. 16).

To serve from freezer Thaw either overnight in the fridge or for about 6 hours at room temperature. If wanted in a hurry, see p. 120. Chopped chives can be added to the thawed salad, also for a more exotic salad, sliced beetroot, chopped nuts and a little Canadian Mayonnaise (p. 168).

Sweet and Sour Cabbage (p. 110)

Braised Red Cabbage (p. 109)

Buttered Carrots (p. 113)

Ratatouille (p. 108)

HERBS

If you can get them during late spring and early summer, herbs that are in general use, such as parsley, mint, thyme and chives, and bouquets garnis—made up with 2 or 3 sprigs parsley, a sprig each rosemary and thyme, and a bay leaf—are well worth freezing. These will keep their fragrance and lovely fresh flavour for months. Tie the individual herbs into bunches, two or three times the size of bouquets garnis. It is most important that herbs should be carefully wrapped so that their pungent odours cannot penetrate other packages. Those with larger freezers usually store herbs in screw-topped bottles; but plenty of clinging film and strong, well-sealed polythene bags should be satisfactory.

An alternative method for freezing herbs like parsley, mint and chives is to chop them very finely and pack firmly with a minimum of water into the compartments of an ice-cube tray. Eject the frozen cubes and pack in a polythene bag for freezing. These are useful for sauces and casseroles.

Fruit

Methods for Freezing Fruit · Fruit Cooked in its own Sweetened Juice

As with vegetables, owners of small freezers can spare only limited storage space for fruit. Yet when fresh summer fruits come their way, some of them, if frozen, would be much appreciated in the bleak months ahead.

Methods for Freezing Fruit

In dry unsweetened packs For soft fruit. Especially good for raspberries and gooseberries. Pack in polythene bags.

In dry sugar packs An alternative for soft, juicy fruit. 1 lb (400 g) fruit, coated with ¼ lb (100 g) sugar and packed in polythene bags.

As a sweetened purée A particularly good method for strawberries, which otherwise tend to lose flavour. Allow sugar as above, and put with fruit in a blender or through a moulin-légumes. Sieve to eliminate splintered pips. Block freeze (p. 16).

In their own sweetened juice This is an excellent way of freezing fruits that are cooked before serving. For details see below.

Fruit Cooked in its own Sweetened Juice

*Oven setting 190°–200° F—88°–93° C—Mark Low or 'S' or Slow Cooking Method**

This very slow method of cooking fruit with sweetening but no extra liquid is, in my opinion, the best way for flavour, colour and

* When other dishes are being cooked by this method (pp. 44–6) fruit can be included. It will come to no harm if left in the oven long after it is actually cooked.

consistency. It is excellent both for immediate serving or for freezing. These fruits are just right for flan and tartlet fillings, see p. 132.

Allow:

5 oz (125 g) sugar, jam or honey to 1 lb (400 g) fruit (apples and pears: peeled, cored and sliced; stone fruit: unpeeled and, if not too hard, stones removed)

Place fruit and sweetening in a casserole with a closely fitting lid and cook in the slow oven until the sugar has dissolved in the exuded fruit juices. The time will vary considerably from 1½ to 3 hours according to the type of fruit. Stir occasionally during the cooking. When cool enough remove any stones.

To freeze Put the fruit and syrup into suitable rectangular containers. Chill and block freeze (p. 16).

To use from freezer Thaw blocks either overnight in fridge or for several hours at room temperature.

Puddings, Sweets, Sweet Sauces and Fillings

Sponge Puddings and Other Sweets · Sweets Made with Pastry · Puff Pastry Slices · Pancakes · Banana and Fruit Sauce Pancakes · Crêpes Suzette · Ice Cream 1 and 2 · Economy Ice Cream—Vanilla or Coffee Flavoured · Ice Cream Desserts · Butterscotch Sauce · Chocolate Butterscotch Sauce · Spice Butterscotch Sauce · Orange Brandy Butterscotch Sauce · Orange or Lemon Syrup · Fresh Fruit Salad · Nut Topping · Fruit and Jelly Fillings · Mock Lemon Curd Filling · Butterscotch Nut Filling · Butterscotch Crunch Fillings

Most owners of small freezers will not have much storage space for puddings or sweets, so will want to make the best use of the little room they can spare. The following suggestions are given with this fact in mind.

Apart from ice creams, the most valuable of freezer sweets, do not freeze complete puddings or sweets, except those made for special occasions. It is wiser to freeze their bases which, with ready-to-hand additions, can soon become the required dishes. A variety of suggestions is given in the sections on Cake Foundation (pp. 134–51) and Pastry (pp. 151–60).

A supply of frozen cream (p. 172) is a good idea. It improves so many sweets, especially ices.

Frozen Custard Cream (p. 174) will also be appreciated. It is delicious with fruit and most welcome when a trifle is to be made.

Sponge Puddings and Other Sweets

A small frozen block of Cake Foundation (p. 134), can easily be made into a hot or cold sweet or a short crust sweet pastry dough (pp. 146–50).

Sweets Made with Pastry

Frozen ready-to-bake pastry cases and pie lids are useful and time-saving. Instructions for making and baking them are given on pp. 157–60. Suggested fillings are on pp. 132–3.

Puff Pastry Slices

Hot or cold they make delicious sweets (p. 160).

Cut them horizontally into three, so you can have two layers of filling—jam, lemon curd or one of the fillings on pp. 132–3—and when a slice of ice cream is incorporated you have a sweet to be proud of. This should be topped with whipped cream.

Pancakes

With a supply of Pancakes (p. 97) in your freezer, delicious hot sweets can be served in next to no time. Suggested pancake sauces and fillings are given on pp. 129–33.

Banana and Fruit Sauce Pancakes

To serve 2 allow:

4 pancakes, heated
½ oz (12·5 g) butter
1 oz (25 g) caster sugar
3 dessertspoons (30 ml) orange juice
1 dessertspoon (10 ml) lemon juice
2 bananas

Melt the butter in a frying pan, add the sugar and fruit juices. Simmer gently until the sugar is dissolved, stirring continuously to prevent burning. Cut the bananas in half lengthwise and place in the pan for a moment to warm through. Lay each half on a hot pancake and roll up. Place on a hot serving dish, pour over the hot sauce and serve.

Crêpes Suzette

To serve 2 allow:

4 pancakes, heated
½ oz (12·5 g) butter
½ oz (12·5 g) caster sugar
juice of ½ an orange
¼ teaspoon (1·25 ml) grated orange rind
¼ teaspoon (1·25 ml) grated lemon rind
2 tablespoons (30 ml) Cointreau, Curaçao, or Grand Marnier
1 tablespoon (15 ml) brandy

Fold the hot pancakes in four. Melt the butter in a frying pan. Add sugar, orange juice, orange and lemon rind and liqueur. Bring to the boil. Add pancakes, heat through, turning twice. Transfer to serving dish, pour over brandy, set alight and serve immediately.

ICE CREAMS

With ice cream in the freezer, we are never at a loss for a sweet. A lot of people rely on bought ice creams, which are usually palatable, even the cheap ones that have no connection with farm produce. Many of us, on the other hand, prefer to make our own ice creams, provided they are really good, not too much trouble and preferably not too expensive. Still, like everything in life, you get what you pay for; so, when you make delicious ice creams with dairy cream and eggs, they won't be cheap, but will cost less than manufactured ones containing similar ingredients. When, however, your ice cream is made from a tin of evaporated milk, it will still be good, though obviously not as good as those real cream ices, yet you will know that your cheap home-made variety is cheaper than its commercial counterpart and is made of milk and not animal fat.

The following two excellent ice creams could not be quicker or more simple to make, yet compare favourably with many much more complicated recipes. Both can be made satisfactorily with Home-made Cream (p. 172). They are very alike, except the first is made with whole eggs and the second with egg whites only. This means that the latter is useful when, as so often happens, the yolks have been used for other purposes. Neither recipe need be beaten a second time during freezing, though if Ice Cream 2 is given a second beating it will become a little creamier, but will also lose considerable bulk.

Do not serve ice cream direct from the freezer, but allow it to soften a little in the fridge for ¼ to 1 hour—exactly how long will depend on the type and quantity. You must learn from experience.

Ice Cream 1

2 eggs, separated
4 tablespoons (60 ml) icing sugar (more if liked)
5 or 6 fluid oz (125 or 150 ml)* double cream
a little vanilla sugar (optional)

Whisk and blend the yolks well in a small basin. Whisk the egg whites in a mixing bowl until very stiff. While still whisking sift in the icing sugar, a teaspoon at a time. Whisk the cream with a wire, not a rotary, whisk until it forms light peaks, then fold it, the egg yolks and vanilla sugar into the egg whites and sugar.

To freeze Turn the mixture into foil or plastic rectangular containers and block freeze (p. 16).

Ice Cream 2

4 egg whites
6 fluid oz (150 ml)* double cream
4 tablespoons (60 ml) icing sugar (more if liked)
a little vanilla sugar (optional)

Whisk the egg white until very stiff. Then, still whisking, add the sugar, a teaspoon at a time. Whisk the cream with a wire, not a rotary, whisk into soft peaks and fold it and the vanilla sugar into the egg white and sugar.

To freeze As given for Ice Cream 1.

Economy Ice Cream—Vanilla or Coffee Flavoured

Before a tin of evaporated milk can be used, it must first be stood, unopened, in a pan of water, boiled for 15 minutes, cooled and then

* Cream is sold in 5 or 6 fluid oz (125 or 150 ml) cartons. Ice Cream 1 can be made with either, but if only 5 fluid oz cartons are obtainable when making Ice Cream 2, use either 4 whites from small eggs or 3 from large ones.

stored in the fridge for at least 24 hours. Those who often make this ice cream should always keep a boiled tin or so in readiness.
When Economy Ice Creams are well flavoured, the milk's distinctive taste can be more or less eradicated and when sauces etc. are also added it can be completely masked.

1¼ teaspoons (6·25 ml) powdered gelatine soaked in 1 tablespoon (15 ml) cold water, or cold coffee
3 tablespoons (45 ml) boiling water, or boiling coffee
a large tin prepared evaporated milk
3 tablespoons (45 ml) caster sugar
1½ teaspoons (7·5 ml) vanilla essence; or Camp coffee to taste

Dissolve the soaked gelatine with the boiling water or coffee. Whip the evaporated milk together with the sugar until it is light, thick and more than twice the original quantity. Towards the end of the whipping, gradually add the dissolved gelatine and the vanilla or Camp coffee.

To freeze Pour the mixture into shallow foil or metal trays and freeze for 30–45 minutes. Remove from freezer, empty the partially frozen ice cream back into the mixing bowl, whip it again, and finally spoon into not too deep foil or plastic rectangular containers. Block freeze (p. 16).

Ice Cream Desserts

With ice cream in the freezer, varied foods at our disposal, imagination and resourcefulness, the delicious desserts we can concoct must be well nigh inexhaustible.
Complementary foods can be incorporated in the ice cream mixture before freezing, for instance:

chopped preserved or crystallized ginger
coarsely crushed nut brittle
broken-up chocolate peppermint crisps
2 oz (50 g) seedless raisins, soaked at least 2 hours in 2 tablespoons (30 ml) rum

This type of ice cream needs a gentle stir as it begins to freeze, to prevent the additions sinking to the bottom.
The ice cream can be a recipe's integral component, as in:

Banana Splits
Pêche Melba
Meringues Glacés (meringues will keep for months in airtight tins)
Puff Pastry Slices (p. 124)
Orange, Strawberry or Raspberry Delights (pp. 148–9)
Ginger Delights (p. 148)

The ice cream can be covered with a sauce or other foods and topped with cream. A few suggestions are given in the following section.

SAUCES, TOPPINGS AND FILLINGS FOR PUDDINGS, PANCAKES, SWEETS AND ICE CREAMS

Butterscotch Sauce

This useful sauce and its variations are good hot on puddings and pancakes, cold on ice cream. It also makes a base for fillings.

3 oz (75 g) butter, or margarine
2 oz (50 g) golden syrup
5 oz (125 g) dark moist sugar
2 fluid oz (50 ml) water
1½ oz (37·5 g) flour
¼ pint (125 ml) milk

Heat, in not too small a saucepan (one with a heavy base), the fat, syrup, sugar and water. Stir until the sugar has dissolved. Then without further stirring, allow to boil for three minutes. Remove from heat. Slowly sieve the flour into the mixture and, while stirring, gradually add the milk. Replace over heat and stir until the sauce thickens.

Pour into a storage container, but do not cover until cold. Butterscotch Sauce will keep for months in a cool dry place and even longer in the fridge.

Chocolate Butterscotch Sauce

Mix together:

1 tablespoon (15 ml) cocoa
3 tablespoons (45 ml) water
2 tablespoons (30 ml) Butterscotch Sauce (p. 129)

Spice Butterscotch Sauce

Mix together:

½ teaspoon (2·5 ml) ground ginger
a pinch of cinnamon
a pinch of mixed spice
2 tablespoons (30 ml) boiling water
2 tablespoons (30 ml) Butterscotch Sauce (p. 129)

Orange Brandy Butterscotch Sauce

Mix together:

grated rind of 1 orange, crushed with a little sugar
4 tablespoons (60 ml) orange juice
3 tablespoons (45 ml) Butterscotch Sauce (p. 129)
1½ tablespoons (22·5 ml) brandy

Orange or Lemon Syrup (made in a liquidizer)

This syrup will keep for weeks. It is good over sponge puddings, pancakes and ice cream and in Fresh Fruit Salad (p. 131).
It is made with:

oranges, or lemons
boiling water
granulated sugar

After removing the pips, cut the whole fruit into small pieces, and place in the liquidizer. Just cover them with boiling water, and blend for 10–15 seconds—not a moment longer. Empty the mixture into a nylon sieve, placed over a measure. (If you have liquidized too long, you will have to drip the liquor through a cloth; the result will be all right, but it's a nuisance.) When the liquor has drained off, pour it into a saucepan, large enough to prevent the syrup from boiling over, and add the same measure of sugar.
Place pan over heat and stir until the sugar has dissolved. Boil rapidly for 2–3 minutes. Pour the syrup into a warmed screw-topped jar or plastic container, and cover when cold. Store in the fridge.

Fresh Fruit Salad

When you have Orange Syrup (p. 130) and any fresh fruit, you can quickly make a fruit salad. It will taste delicious, and the syrup prevents the fruit from discolouring. The salad can be served with ice cream, cream, custard cream or in a trifle or as a filling for pastry cases.
For parties a little sherry, brandy, one of the orange liqueurs or maraschino can be added.
Any surplus fruit salad can be block frozen (p. 16).

Nut Topping

This is nice sprinkled over ice cream sundaes, etc., and is made with:

mixed chopped nuts (these can be bought in packets)
butter and sugar

Fry the nuts a golden brown in hot butter. Sprinkle with plenty of sugar and fry a further few minutes. Spread the nuts on absorbent paper to cool. Store in an airtight container.

Fruit and Jelly Fillings

For Pastry Cases (p. 157). These must be prepared and set well in advance of serving. The fruit is either tinned, fresh or Fruit Cooked in its own Sweetened Juice (p. 122).
The fillings are set either in foil cases similar to those over which the pastry was or is to be baked or, for Vol-au-Vent Flans, in the sandwich tin used for cutting out the flan centre (p. 160).
Arrange the fruit (if tinned or cooked, previously strained) in appropriate containers, and estimate the amount of jelly required. To each ¼ pint (125 ml) liquid allow 1 teaspoon (5 ml) powdered gelatine.

With fresh fruit the liquid is Water and a little seedless jam, to give flavour and colour; or half sweet sherry or sweet red wine and half water.
The jam must be added to the liquid when boiling. It can also be used with the alcohol mixture.

With tinned or cooked fruit the liquid is The fruit syrup, if necessary increased with a little sherry, wine or water

Put the gelatine in a cup and pour over it a little of the cold liquid—just enough to cover the gelatine—and leave to soak for a few minutes. Boil up the remaining liquid and pour it over the soaked gelatine. Stir well until the gelatine is completely dissolved before pouring the jelly over the arranged fruit.

Mock Lemon Curd Filling (p. 151)

For Pastry Cases (p. 157), Pastry Slices (p. 124) and Pancakes (p. 97).

Butterscotch Nut Filling

For Pastry Cases (p. 157).
Fill cases with Butterscotch Sauce (p. 129) covered with Nut Topping (p. 181).

Butterscotch Crunch Fillings

Cold in Pastry Cases (p. 157), hot in Pancakes (p. 97).
To each tablespoon (15 ml) Butterscotch Sauce (p. 129) allow 2 digestive biscuits. Crumble the biscuits and mix with the sauce. This filling is nice as it is, but more interesting with the addition of one or more of the following:

chopped nuts
chopped preserved ginger (including a little syrup)
chopped dates
glacé cherries

Cake Foundation—the Base for Cakes, Scones, Biscuits, Sponge Puddings Sweet Short Pastry and Mock Lemon Curd

Cake Foundation · Standard Sponge · Standard Sponge Small Cakes · Fruit Buns · Small Chocolate Cakes · Small Orange Cakes · Queen Cakes · Small Cherry Cakes · Small Fruit Cakes · Small Rice Cakes · Madeira Cake · Orange Cake · Pain de Gênes · Sultana Cake · Treacle Fruit Cake · Rich Fruit Cake · Rich Cherry Cake · Scones · Almond Biscuits · Vienna Biscuits · Great-Grandmother's Chocolate Biscuits · Shrewsbury Biscuits · Continental Sugar Biscuits · Shortcrust Biscuits · Ginger Snaps · Peanut Nibbles · Cheese Nibbles · Sponge Puddings and Toppings · Pineapple Plaisance · Ginger Delights · Orange Delights · Strawberry or Raspberry Delights · Strawberry or Raspberry Shortcake · Copenhagen Fruit Pie · Cake Foundation Pastry · Cake Foundation Mock Lemon Curd

There are many people who do not habitually keep fresh cakes, but do appreciate the odd cake for guests or have an occasional appetite for them themselves.

Space for a selection of cakes can usually be found in larger freezers, but is not practical in small ones. For these the answer may well be small frozen blocks of Cake Foundation. These take up far less space, yet can quickly and easily be turned into a large choice of cakes or any of those given on p. 133.
Cake Foundation is simply blended soft margarine or butter, sugar and eggs. All the recipe's remaining ingredients are added just before baking. If the frozen blocks are placed in a mixing bowl in the newly switched on oven, after about five minutes they should be sufficiently soft for the recipe's completion, and ready for baking as soon as the oven is hot enough.

CAKE FOUNDATION AND HOW TO USE IT

½ lb (200 g) soft margarine or softened butter
½ lb (200 g) caster sugar
2 eggs, weighing about 4 oz (100 g), well beaten

Beat the shortening and sugar and when light and creamy, gradually beat in the eggs.

The Foundation can now be either:

1. Used.
2. Stored in a cool place for up to three weeks, provided the eggs are genuinely 'new laid'.
3. Frozen into four 5 oz (125 g) blocks (p. 16). Each small block will contain: 2 oz (50 g) shortening, 2 oz (50 g) sugar and ½ an egg.

Apart from recipes especially contrived for Cake Foundation, any recipe can be used that includes no less than: 4 oz (100 g) shortening, 4 oz (100 g) sugar and 1 egg.

These ingredients make up 10 oz (250 g) Cake Foundation; or two 5 oz (125 g) frozen blocks.

You arrive at the same recipe by adding to 10 oz (250 g) Cake Foundation, or two 5 oz (125 g) blocks, all the ingredients over and above 4 oz (100 g) shortening, 4 oz (100 g) sugar and 1 egg. For example, here is a comparison between the recipe for an orthodox Victoria Sandwich and the same recipe made with Cake Foundation.

Orthodox Sandwich	*Cake Foundation Sandwich*
4 oz (100 g) margarine, or butter	10 oz (250 g) Cake Foundation; or two 5 oz (125 g) blocks
4 oz (100 g) caster sugar	1 egg
2 eggs	4 oz (100 g) self-raising flour
4 oz (100 g) self-raising flour	1 tablespoon (15 ml) warm water
1 tablespoon (15 ml) warm water	

How, and in which order, to incorporate the ingredients which, according to the recipe, must be added to Cake Foundation

1. *Shortening* Additional shortening is beaten into the soft Cake Foundation. Should the former be hard, it can join the frozen Foundation for the last minutes in the heating oven (p. 134).

2. *Sugar, Eggs, Ground Almonds, Treacle, Jam, Marmalade, Orange or Lemon Juice or Grated Peel* These are beaten into the creamed Cake Foundation with a fork or a wire or perforated spoon.

3. *Dried Fruit, Preserved or Crystallized Ginger, Nuts, Coconut, Rolled Oats, Chocolate Lumps* These are lightly folded into the mixture with a metal spoon.

4. *Flour, Raising Agents, Spices, Salt, Cocoa, Ground Rice, Cornflour* These should be sifted at least once. When you feel conscientious, or for extra lightness, sift three times.

For light mixtures: fold the flour etc. gently into the other ingredients with a large metal spoon.

For dough-like mixtures, e.g. scones: work it in with a palette knife or perforated spoon.

5. *Liquids* For light mixtures: gradually add together with the flour, etc.
For dough-like mixtures, e.g. scones: the liquid is added after the flour has been worked into the Foundation. A palette or pliable knife is good for the job.

CAKES AND SCONES

Standard Sponge

1 small block Cake Foundation (p. 134)
5 rounded dessertspoons (60 ml) self-raising flour
sufficient liquid to enable the batter to drop from the spoon: this may be milk; milk and water; milk and fruit juice (or squash); neat fruit juice; squash; or syrup

Standard Sponge batter is most useful. In a matter of moments it can be turned into small cakes, or a variety of puddings and sweets (pp. 146–9).

Standard Sponge Small Cakes

Oven setting 400° F—200° C—Mark 6

Standard Sponge, as above; with a choice of flavours and additions

Suggested flavours vanilla, orange, lemon, coffee, chocolate, powdered ginger, cinnamon, mixed spice.

Suggested additions dried fruit, glacé cherries, nuts, preserved or crystallized ginger, caraway seeds, chocolate drops.

Blend the additional ingredients with the Cake Foundation and half fill small oiled foil or metal cases or tins or unoiled parchment baking cases with the mixture.
Bake 10–15 minutes in preheated oven.

Fruit Buns *Oven setting 400° F—200° C—Mark 6*

1 small block Cake Foundation (p. 134)
1½ oz (37·5 g) butter, or margarine
4 oz (100 g) currants and sultanas
6 oz (150 g) plain flour
a good pinch of bicarbonate of soda
a good pinch of mixed spice
½ teaspoon (2·5 ml) vanilla (optional)

Blend the additional ingredients with the Cake Foundation. Put small rough heaps of the mixture on to a greased, floured sheet. Bake 10–15 minutes, or till brown, in preheated oven.

Small Chocolate Cakes *Oven setting 400° F—200° C—Mark 6*

1 small block Cake Foundation (p. 134)
1 oz (25 g) butter, or margarine
1 oz (25 g) caster sugar
2 oz (50 g) chopped walnuts (optional)
5 oz (125 g) self-raising flour
1 oz (25 g) ground rice
3 dessertspoons (30 ml) chocolate powder
a little strong coffee

Blend the additional ingredients with the Cake Foundation, and spoon the mixture into small oiled foil cases or metal tins or unoiled parchment baking cases. Bake 10–15 minutes in preheated oven. When cold, cover with chocolate icing or chocolate couverture.

Small Orange Cakes *Oven setting 400° F—200° C—Mark 6*

1 small block Cake Foundation (p. 134)
1 tablespoon (15 ml) marmalade
grated rind of 1 small orange, crushed with a dessertspoon (10 ml) caster sugar
4 oz (100 g) self-raising flour
the orange juice

Blend the additional ingredients with the Cake Foundation. Spoon the mixture into small oiled foil cases or metal tins or unoiled parchment baking cases. Bake 10–15 minutes in preheated oven.

Queen Cakes *Oven setting 350° F—180° C—Mark 4*

1 small block Cake Foundation (p. 134)
1 oz (25 g) butter, or margarine
1 oz (25 g) caster sugar
1 egg
4 oz (100 g) plain flour
½ teaspoon (2·5 ml) baking powder
pinch of salt
1 tablespoon (15 ml) milk, and if liked, a little vanilla essence

Blend the additional ingredients with the Cake Foundation. Spoon the mixture into small oiled foil cases or metal tins or unoiled parchment baking cases. Bake about 15 minutes in preheated oven.

Small Cherry Cakes *Oven setting 350° F—180° C—Mark 4*

As for Queen Cakes with the addition of 3–4 oz (75–100 g) glacé cherries.

Small Fruit Cakes *Oven setting 350° F—180° C—Mark 4*

As for Queen Cakes with the addition of 4 oz (100 g) mixed fruit and, if liked, a little mixed spice.

Small Rice Cakes *Oven setting 350° F—180° C—Mark 4*

1 small block Cake Foundation (p. 134)
1 oz (25 g) butter, or margarine
1 oz (25 g) caster sugar
1 egg
2½ oz (62·5 g) plain flour

1½ oz (37·5 g) ground rice
½ teaspoon (2·5 ml) baking powder
a little milk and lemon juice to mix

Blend the additional ingredients with the Cake Foundation. Spoon the mixture into small oiled foil cases or metal tins or unoiled parchment baking cases. Bake about 15 minutes in preheated oven.

Madeira Cake *Oven setting 325° F—170° C—Mark 3*

Double the ingredients given for Queen Cakes (p. 138). Spoon the batter into a greased 7 in (18 cm) cake tin. Bake 1½–1¾ hours in preheated oven.

Orange Cake *Oven setting 350° F—180° C—Mark 4*

Double the ingredients given for Small Orange Cakes (p. 137). Spoon the mixture into a greased 7 in (18 cm) cake or 2 lb (1 kilo) loaf tin. Bake 1 hour in preheated oven.

Pain de Gênes *Oven setting 350° F—180° C—Mark 4*

This cake may be extravagant, but is extremely good.

1 small block Cake Foundation (p. 134)
3 oz (75 g) caster sugar
2 eggs beaten alternately with:
  2½ oz (62·5 g) ground almonds
  1½ oz (37·5 g) plain flour
3 teaspoons (15 ml) kirsch (optional)

Blend additional ingredients with the Cake Foundation. Spoon the mixture into a 8 in (20 cm) sandwich tin with greased or Bakewell paper on the bottom. Bake in preheated oven for about 1 hour, lowering the heat a little after the first ½ hour.

Sultana Cake *Oven setting 350° F—180° C—Mark 4*

1 small block Cake Foundation (p. 134)
2 oz (50 g) butter, or margarine
1 oz (25 g) caster sugar
1 egg
¼ lb (100 g) sultanas
1 oz (25 g) candied peel
½ lb (200 g) plain flour
1 teaspoon (5 ml) baking powder
2½ fluid oz (62·5 ml) milk or sherry

Blend the additional ingredients with the Cake Foundation. Spoon the mixture into a well-greased 7 in (18 cm) cake or 2 lb (1 kilo) loaf tin. Bake in preheated oven for 1½ hours, reducing heat after first half-hour to 325° F—170° C—Mark 3.

Treacle Fruit Cake *Oven setting 350° F—180° C—Mark 4*

1 small block Cake Foundation (p. 134)
2 oz (50 g) butter, or margarine
1 egg
2 oz (50 g) golden syrup, or treacle
3 oz (75 g) currants
2 oz (50 g) sultanas
1 oz (25 g) candied peel
½ lb (200 g) plain flour
1 teaspoon (5 ml) bicarbonate of soda
2 tablespoons (30 ml) milk

Blend the additional ingredients with the Cake Foundation. Spoon the mixture into a greased 7 in (18 cm) cake or 2 lb (1 kilo) loaf tin. Bake in preheated oven 1¼–1½ hours, reducing the heat to 325° F—170° C—Mark 3 after the first half-hour.

Rich Fruit Cake *Oven setting 350° F—180° C—Mark 4*

A delicious cake which can be cut the day after baking or kept quite a long time in an airtight tin. The cake is not large, and as it is suitable for any occasion, including Christmas, can be doubled when a larger cake is wanted.

1 small block Cake Foundation (p. 134)
3 oz (75 g) butter, or margarine
3 oz (75 g) soft brown sugar
1 egg
the grated rind of one small lemon
2 oz (50 g) each: raisins, cherries and candied peel
4 oz (100 g) sultanas
6 oz (150 g) currants
6½ oz (162·5 g) plain flour
¼ teaspoon (1·25 ml) each, ground nutmeg and mixed spice
¼ teaspoon (1·25 ml) bicarbonate of soda dissolved in a little warm milk

Blend the additional ingredients with the Cake Foundation. Spoon the mixture into a well-greased cake tin with greased paper on the bottom. Bake in preheated oven for 3 hours. After the first 20 minutes, reduce heat gradually to 300° F—150° C—Mark 2, or lower if the cake is cooking too quickly.

Rich Cherry Cake *Oven setting 350° F—180° C—Mark 4*

As given for Rich Fruit Cake, except the frut and peel are replaced by 1 lb (400 g) glacé cherries, and the nutmeg and mixed spice by a little vanilla or lemon essence.

Scones

When Cake Foundation is available, it takes far less time to prepare scones than it does to heat the oven to 425° F—220° C—Mark 7.

1 small block Cake Foundation (p. 134)
12½ oz (312·5 g) self-raising flour
milk or whey to mix

This should make about 24 scones. When fewer are wanted, either halve or quarter the recipe.

Another method is to allow For each heaped spoon (any spoon) of Cake Foundation, 5 rounded spoons (the same spoon) self-raising flour. A tablespoon (15 ml spoon) should make 6 medium-sized scones.

Work the flour into the thawed Foundation with a fork or a perforated spoon. Then with a palette knife or a pliable kitchen knife, mix in just enough liquid to make a moist but easily handled dough. Turn this dough on to a well-floured baking sheet. Pat it out with your hands to a thickness of about ¾ in (2 cm) and cut out the scones —all on the baking sheet. Bake in preheated oven for 8–10 minutes.

BISCUITS

A small block of Cake Foundation can be turned quickly and easily into over ½ lb (200 g) of delicious home-made biscuits. These are not likely to last long, but if need be will keep fresh for months in an air-tight tin.

Almond Biscuits

Oven setting 400° F—200° C—Mark 6

1 small block Cake Foundation (p. 134)
2 oz (50 g) ground almonds
¼ lb (100 g) plain flour

Knead the mixture into a dough. Either roll out thinly and cut into shapes, or form into little balls by hand and flatten these on the greased baking sheet. Bake 10–15 minutes in preheated oven.

Vienna Biscuits *Oven setting 400° F—200° C—Mark 6*

1 small block Cake Foundation (p. 134)
2 oz (50 g) caster sugar
3½ oz (87·5 g) plain flour
¾ teaspoon (3·75 ml) cream of tartar
a pinch of bicarbonate of soda
¼ teaspoon (1.25 ml) cinnamon
only if necessary, a very little milk

Knead into a dough, and roll out thinly. Cut into rounds or fancy shapes—on the small side, as these biscuits spread considerably. Place not too closely on a greased baking sheet. Bake about 10 minutes in preheated oven.
These make good chocolate biscuits if covered, when cold, with chocolate courverture.

Great-Grandmother's Chocolate Biscuits *Oven setting 400° F—200° C—Mark 6*

1 small block Cake Foundation (p. 134)
2 oz (50 g) bar plain chocolate, finely grated
1 oz (25 g) ground almonds
4 oz (100 g) plain flour
pinch of mixed spice

Roll dough to a thickness of ¼ in (½ cm) and cut into fancy shapes, or roll into little balls and flatten on the greased baking sheet to the same thickness. Either brush with egg white and decorate with split blanched almonds, or when cold after baking cover with chocolate couverture. Bake about 15 minutes or until a pale brown.

Shrewsbury Biscuits *Oven setting 325° F—170° C—Mark 3*

1 small block Cake Foundation (p. 134)
½ teaspoon (2·5 ml) caraway seeds

3 oz (75 g) plain flour
¼ teaspoon (1·25 ml) cinnamon

Knead the mixture well. Either roll out and cut into shapes, or form into balls and flatten into rounds on the greased sheet. Bake in preheated oven for about 30 minutes.

Continental Sugar Biscuits *Oven setting 400° F—200° C—Mark 6*

This recipe makes about 1 lb (400 g) of biscuits.

1 small block Cake Foundation (p. 134)
2 oz (50 g) butter, or margarine
2 oz (50 g) caster sugar
grated rind of 1 lemon
1 oz (25 g) ground almonds
½ lb (200 g) plain flour
a little vanilla

Knead the mixture and roll out thinly. Cut into biscuits. Bake on well-greased sheet in preheated oven for about 10 minutes.
These biscuits, when cold, are good covered with chocolate couverture.

Shortcrust Biscuits *Oven setting 350° F—180° C—Mark 4*

Cake Foundation Pastry (p. 150) is used for these good, quick to make biscuits. The dough should be flavoured according to taste, rolled out thinly and cut into biscuits. Bake 10–15 minutes on greased baking sheet in preheated oven.

Ginger Snaps *Oven setting 375° F—190° C—Mark 5*

These crisp spicy biscuits taste as much of cloves as they do of ginger; those who think too much so, should reduce the cloves and perhaps increase the ginger.

1 small block Cake Foundation (p. 134)
1 oz (25 g) butter, or margarine
1 oz (25 g) caster sugar
2½ tablespoons (37·5 ml) black treacle
1 egg
¼ lb (100 g) plain flour
1 teaspoon (5 ml) baking powder
1 teaspoon (5 ml) ground ginger
½–1 teaspoon (2·5–5 ml) ground cloves
1 teaspoon (5 ml) cinnamon

Mix all the ingredients. Using two teaspoons, drop little lumps of the dough into a small bowl of caster sugar. Still using the spoons, roll the little lumps in the sugar and gently form them into balls. Place these 3 in (8 cm) apart on baking sheets covered with Bakewell, or very well greased. Bake about 15 minutes in preheated oven.
Ginger Snaps are used in Ginger Delights (p. 148).

Peanut Nibbles *Oven setting 350° F—180° C—Mark 4*

These are delicious and unusual. The salted peanuts are easily ground in an electric grinder or liquidizer or passed through a hand shredder or mincer. They make good cocktail biscuits.

1 small block Cake Foundation (p. 134)
2½ oz (62·5 g) butter, or margarine
10 oz (250 g) salted peanuts (not too finely ground)
2½ tablespoons (37·5 ml) finely grated parmesan
5 oz (125 g) plain flour
a pinch of cayenne
salt and pepper to taste

Knead the dough and either roll it out thinly, cut into small shapes and place on a baking sheet, or form the dough by hand into little balls, place these on the baking sheet and flatten them with your hands or the bottom of a milk bottle. Bake for 10 to 15 minutes in preheated oven.

Cheese Nibbles *Oven setting 350° F—180° C—Mark 4*

These are useful, as the prepared dough is frozen and the Nibbles baked either after 24 hours or several months in the freezer.

1 small block Cake Foundation, just thawed (p. 134)
2½ oz (62·5 g) butter, or margarine, not too hard
5 oz (125 g) finely grated cheese, cheddar type
2½ tablespoons (37·5 ml) finely grated parmesan
5 oz (125 g) plain flour
1 teaspoon (5 ml) dry mustard
a pinch of cayenne
salt and pepper to taste

Form the dough into rolls about 1½ in (4 cm) in diameter, wrap them in clinging film and place in the freezer. After 24 hours, either pack the rolls in polythene bags, seal and return to the freezer, for future baking, or cut frozen rolls into slices, as thin as possible, and place on a cold baking sheet. Bake in preheated oven for 10 to 15 minutes. Nice served with drinks.

PUDDINGS AND SWEETS

Sponge Puddings *Oven setting 375° F—190° C—Mark 5*

To serve 2 use a Standard Sponge batter made from a small block of Cake Foundation (p. 136) suitably flavoured with lemon, orange, vanilla or chocolate powder. Put the chosen topping from the following recipes on the bottom of a greased oven dish and cover with sponge batter. Bake in a preheated oven 20 minutes or until the sponge is cooked.

To serve Turn out on to a hot dish, with the sauce or fruit on top.

The Toppings

Treacle Sponge Pudding

½ oz (12·5 g) melted butter, or margarine
2 tablespoons (30 ml) brown sugar
2 tablespoons (30 ml) golden syrup
juice of ½ lemon (optional)

Jam or Marmalade Sponge Pudding

5 tablespoons (75 ml) jam, or marmalade
2 tablespoons (30 ml) water

Butterscotch Sponge Pudding

3–4 tablespoons (45–60 ml) Butterscotch Sauce (p. 129)

Chocolate Sponge Pudding

3–4 tablespoons (45–60 ml) Chocolate Butterscotch Sauce (p. 130)

Fruit Sponge Pudding

1 oz (25 g) melted butter, or margarine
4 tablespoons (60 ml) sugar, more if liked
about ½ lb (200 g) fresh fruit, or rhubarb (hard fruit: peeled, cored and cut up; stoned fruit: stones removed)

Pineapple Plaisance

Oven setting 375° F—190° C—Mark 5

4½ in (11 cm) foil dishes are needed for this popular recipe.
To serve 4 allow:

4 knobs of butter, or margarine
4 tablespoons (60 ml) granulated sugar
4 slices tinned pineapple
8 glacé cherries, chopped
pineapple syrup
a little rum, sherry, or orange liqueur (optional)
Standard Sponge batter made with a small block of Cake Foundation (p. 136) and moistened with pineapple syrup.

Place a knob of butter or margarine in each dish and melt it in the oven. Cover the melted fat with sugar and place a slice of pineapple on top. Fill the hole with cherries and pour over a little pineapple syrup, laced if liked with alcohol. Cover the pineapple with sponge batter. Bake in preheated oven 10–15 minutes.
Turn out and serve with the pineapple on top.

Ginger Delights

Immediately before serving, these exellent sweets are quickly assembled in individual fruit bowls.

For each Delight allow:

- 2 Ginger Snaps (p. 144)
- a slice of Ice Cream (pp. 126–8)
- about 2 tablespoons (30 ml) ginger syrup, or Spice Butterscotch Sauce (p. 130)
- whipped cream
- a few pieces chopped preserved ginger.

Place the ice cream between the Ginger Snaps. Pour over the syrup or sauce and top with cream and ginger.

Orange Delights

Oven setting 400° F—200° C—Mark 6

For 4 Delights allow:

- Standard Sponge batter made with a small block of Cake Foundation (p. 136)
- 12 tablespoons (120 ml) orange juice
- 3 tablespoons (30 ml) orange liqueur, rum, or brandy (optional)
- 6 orange slices, cut horizontally, pips and pith removed
- 6 slices Ice Cream (pp. 126–8)
- whipping cream

Orange Delights are nicer eaten freshly baked.

Shortly before serving, put the sponge batter into 4 small well-oiled foil baking cases. Bake 10–15 minutes in preheated oven.
Cool the cakes, then split in halves. Put the bottom halves split sides uppermost into individual serving bowls. Mix the orange juice and alcohol (if used) and pour half the liquid over the cake bottoms. Place the orange slices on top, then the Ice Cream. Cover with the cake top halves and pour over the remaining liquid. Decorate with whipped cream and serve.

Strawberry or Raspberry Delights

These are made the same way as Orange Delights, except sherry is used instead of orange juice and spirit, crushed fruit instead of the orange slices, and whole strawberries or raspberries are piled on top of the whipped cream.

Strawberry or Raspberry Shortcake

Oven setting 400° F—200° C—Mark 6

A simple and delicious Cake Foundation version of this classic favourite from the U.S.A.

To serve 4–5 allow:

For the dough:

- a small block Cake Foundation (p. 134)
- 7½ oz (187·5 g) plain flour
- 2½ teaspoons (12·5 ml) cornflour
- 2½ teaspoons (12·5 ml) baking powder
- 2½ fluid oz (62·5 ml) milk

Also required:

- 1 lb (400 g) strawberries, or raspberries
- sugar to taste
- ¼ pint (125 ml) whipping cream

Mix and knead the dough and press it into an 8 in (20 cm) sandwich tin. Bake 10–12 minutes in preheated oven. When cooked, immediatly split shortcake in half.
Crush about three-quarters of the fruit with a fork and mix in the sugar. When the steam has escaped, sandwich the cake halves together with the crushed fruit filling. Just before serving, top with whipped cream and decorate with the remaining fruit.

Copenhagen Fruit Pie *Oven setting 350° F—180° C—Mark 4*

To serve 4–5 allow:

about 1 lb (400 g) fruit, stewed or bottled
1 small block of Cake Foundation (p. 134)
3 egg yolks
1½ oz (37·5 g) plain flour
¼ teaspoon (1·25 ml) salt
½ teaspoon (2·5 ml) bicarbonate of soda
12 fluid oz (300 ml) milk
3 well-whisked egg whites

Place in an oven dish a good layer of fruit with very little juice. Put the Foundation into a basin and beat in the egg yolks. Sieve together the flour, salt and bicarbonate, and stir this into the mixture. When well blended, gradually stir in the milk. Finally fold in the whisked egg whites and pour the batter over the fruit. Bake in preheated oven ¾ hour.
This pudding is nice served hot, but even better cold, when the custard that forms between the fruit and the spongy crust becomes thicker and creamier.

Cake Foundation Pastry *Oven setting 350° F—180° C—Mark 4*

Cake Foundation can be used as a base for a nice sweet shortcrust pastry. Of all the pastry doughs this is the quickest to prepare.
For 1 small block of Cake Foundation (p. 134) allow:

10 level dessertspoons (100 ml) self-raising flour

Work the just thawed Foundation into the flour with a wire or perforated spoon. Knead the mixture well, if necessary sifting in a little extra flour.
Once the dough is made, it can be rolled, shaped and baked, or kept in bulk in the fridge for about a week, or stored in the freezer, without delay, either in slabs or rolled out and cut into shapes.
As the dough is very short and brittle, it may be found easier to handle if rolled out on a piece of floured greaseproof paper.
(See Shortcrust Biscuits, p 144.)

Cake Foundation Mock Lemon Curd

Ingredients:

1 small frozen block Cake Foundation (p. 134), thawed
1 oz (25 g) caster sugar
1 oz (25 g) soft vegetable margarine
grated rind of 1 lemon, crushed in 1 tablespoon (15 ml) sugar
2 eggs, well beaten
juice of 1 lemon

Gradually beat the other ingredients into the soft Cake Foundation. Place the mixture over boiling water, either in the top of a double saucepan or in a basin that fits over a saucepan. Stir until the curd thickens. Use or put into a covered container. The curd will keep in the fridge for well over a month.
This quick, easy to make recipe is excellent in sponge sandwiches, on top of cakes, in Pastry Cases (p. 157), Puff Pastry Slices (p. 160) and Pancakes (p. 97).

Pastry

General Purpose Shortcrust Pastry Dough · Sweet Shortcrust Dough · Puff Pastry Dough · Rough Puff or Flaky Pastry Dough · Flan and Tartlet Cases · Orthodox Vol-au-Vent Cases · Square Vol-au-Vent Cases · Vol-au-Vent Flan Cases · Puff Pastry Slices

All pastries and doughs, baked or unbaked, freeze well. However, with small freezers, it is advisable and space-saving to freeze unbaked pastry, except for savoury flans like Quiche Lorraine.
The uncooked dough can be: (a) rolled out and shaped into pastry cases (including vol-au-vents), pastry slices, pie-dish tops, etc., or used for making sausage rolls, pasties and pies. (b) Formed into slabs.
Whereas the shaped dough and prepared pastry dishes can go straight from the freezer into the newly switched on oven, the slabs of dough cannot be used until they begin to thaw out—about 3 hours at room temperature or overnight in the fridge.

General Purpose Shortcrust Pastry Dough *Oven setting 400° F—200° C—Mark 6*

- 8 oz (200 g) plain flour
- 4 oz (100 g) butter, or soft American style margarine
- 1 egg yolk
- 2 tablespoons (30 ml) cold water

Rub the fat into the flour. Beat the yolk with the water and work the mixture into the flour and fat. Knead until very pliable.

To use without freezing Wrap dough in greaseproof paper and chill in the fridge before using.

To freeze Shape chilled dough into pastry cases (p. 157), pie lids, pasties, etc., or into slabs. Pack, seal and freeze.

To use from freezer Place shaped dough in cold oven and bake as for unfrozen recipes, but allow 8–10 minutes longer, if necessary reducing the heat. Only just thaw slabs of frozen dough before using.

Sweet Shortcrust Dough *Oven setting 400° F—200° C—Mark 6*

This dough is quickly made, freezes well and the pastry is excellent for pies, tarts and pastry cases.

- ½ lb (200 g) lard, warmed (soft, but not melted)
- 4 fluid oz (100 ml) boiling water

1 egg yolk
3 oz (75 g) caster sugar
12 oz (300 g) plain flour

Put the lard, cut into about 6 pieces, into a mixing bowl. Pour the boiling water over it. Immediately stir energetically with a wooden or perforated spoon and at the same time press the fat against the sides of the bowl until the water and fat have fused into a creamy mixture. Beat in the egg yolk and sugar. Sift the flour into the bowl and work it into the other ingredients with a palette or flexible knife.
At this stage, leave the bowl in the fridge for several hours, or if more convenient overnight. Then dredge with flour and knead well with floured hands, until you have a good pliable dough. All this can be done in the mixing bowl. The dough can now be used or frozen.

To freeze Shape dough into pastry cases (p. 157), pie lids, etc., or into slabs. Pack, seal and freeze.

To use from freezer Place shaped dough in a cold oven and bake as for unfrozen recipes, but allow 8–10 minutes longer, if necessary reducing heat. Only just thaw slabs before using.

Note Another good sweet shortcrust pastry can be made with Cake Foundation. This is given on p. 150.

Puff Pastry Dough *Oven setting 475° F—240° C—Mark 9*

Excellent puff pastry doughs are on the market and are a good buy when pressed for time. However, the recipe given is quick and easy to make and considerably cheaper. If possible use strong bread flour, though the pastry is still excellent when ordinary plain flour is used. The secret of good flaky pastries is certainly not lightness of hand—the dough thrives on rough treatment. Success depends on temperature and the ability to form the dough into layers of a plain dough, fat and air. Bear this in mind when following the directions and you can't go wrong.

Use:

equal quantities of strong plain flour and fat
a pinch of salt and very little icy cold water

The fat must consist of:

1 part butter, or a good margarine
3 parts hard English, or Danish lard (never use American as it is much too soft)

The smallest quantities to manage easily are:

½ lb (200 g) flour
2 oz (50 g) butter
6 oz (150 g) lard

The largest recommended quantities are:

1½ lb (600 g) flour
6 oz (150 g) butter
1 lb 2 oz (450 g) lard

Leave the lard in the fridge until the moment it is needed.

1. Sift the flour and salt into a large mixing bowl.
2. Cut or grate the butter or margarine into it.
3. Rub this fat into the flour, using thumbs and fingertips to start with, then the palms of your hands, and at the same time lifting the mixture and showering it back into the bowl. This helps to aerate.
4. With one hand dribble icy cold water, from a cup or small jug, all round the inside rim of the bowl. With the other hand, rotate a fork in the mixture in small circles, working in the water and at the same time forming the dough into rough looking sections. The dough must be pliable yet not too moist. Experience will soon show how much water is needed.
5. With your hands, mould the sections into one lump.
6. Place the dough on to a well-floured working surface and knead it for about 2 minutes.
7. Roll it out to a thickness of about ¼ in (½ cm).

8. Lay the lard, straight out of the fridge, on the centre of the dough.
9. Fold the dough round the lard, pressing the edges firmly together so that the lard is completely enclosed.
10. Here the rough treatment is necessary, and for it you want an easily gripped wooden rolling pin. Raise this well above your shoulder and bang it down—crash, wallop—on top of the dough until it and the lard are flattened out.
11. Now using the rolling pin conventionally, roll the dough into an oblong about $\frac{1}{4}$ in ($\frac{1}{2}$ cm) thick.
12. Make it into a sort of envelope, by folding the front third over the centre third, and the back third over them both. Press the open edges to contain the air. Turn the dough to leave the closed side on the right.
13. Rib and roll alternately, until the dough is once more an oblong. (Ribbing is pressing the rolling pin on to the dough at regular intervals, making a switch-back effect.)
14 to 23. Repeat 12 and 13 five times.
24. Repeat 12 once.

If during these last stages you are unfortunate and find the fat oozing out of the dough, either because the lard was not cold enough, or the kitchen too hot, stop the operation, put the dough in the fridge and leave until sufficiently cold before completing the process.

To use without freezing Wrap the dough in greaseproof paper or put it in an empty flour bag and store in the fridge until the following day. It keeps well for about 3 days.
To get the best out of unfrozen puff pastry, switch on your oven well before the dough comes out of the fridge; and once it has been fashioned, return it to the fridge for a short spell. Then put it on to a cold baking sheet and into a preheated oven. Bake about 10 minutes or until cooked and well risen.

To freeze Wrap, and chill dough in the fridge until the next day. Then (a) shape dough into Vol-au-Vents or other cases, or Pastry Slices (pp. 157–60). (b) Make into Sausage Rolls (p. 94), Pasties (p. 95), mince pies, etc. (c) Leave the dough in slabs. Pack, seal and freeze.

To use from freezer Place frozen shaped or fashioned dough on a cold baking sheet in a cold oven. Bake about 15 minutes or until cooked and well risen. Thaw frozen slabs either in the fridge overnight or 3 hours at room temperature. They must be used when only just thawed.

Rough Puff or Flaky Pastry Dough *Oven setting 450° F—230° C—Mark 8*

This satisfactory flaky pastry is as useful as it is easy to prepare. It is made with:

a good quality cooking fat—any weight from ¼ to 1 lb (100 to 400 g) plain flour—double the chosen weight of fat
a pinch of salt
a little cold water

The smallest quantities to manage easily are:

¼ lb (100 g) fat and ½ lb (200 g) flour

The largest recommended quantities are:

1 lb (½ kilo) fat and 2 lb (1 kilo) flour

The fat must be cold and hard.
1. Sift the flour and salt into a large mixing bowl.
2. Cut the fat into the flour, in pieces of roughly 1 oz (25 g).
3. With one hand, dribble cold water from a cup or small jug all round the inside rim of the bowl. With the other hand, rotate a fork in the mixture in small circles, working in the water, and at the same time forming the dough into rough-looking sections. Do not use more water than necessary or the dough will become too moist.
4. With your hands, mould the sections into one lump.
5. Place the dough on a well-floured working surface.
6. Here, as with puff, heavy-handed treatment is necessary, and for it you need an easily gripped wooden rolling pin. Raise this well

above your shoulder and bang it down on top of the dough until it is flattened out. Now proceed as given for Puff Pastry, stages 11 to 24 (p. 155).

To use without freezing The dough can now be used, or when wrapped in greaseproof paper or put in an empty flour bag will keep up to ten days in the fridge.

To freeze Either (a) roll out dough and cut into shapes for Pastry Cases (*see below*), or pie lids. (b) Use for Pasties (p. 95), etc. Or (c) Leave dough in slabs. Pack, seal and freeze.

To use from freezer Place shaped or fashioned dough onto a cold baking sheet in a cold oven set as above. Bake as for unfrozen dough, allowing a few minutes longer. Thaw slabs of dough in the fridge overnight or about 3 hours at room temperature.

Flan and Tartlet Cases

Pastry cases can be made with any type of pastry dough—home-made or bought. When cases are baked blind, metal or foil cases are usually lined with the dough and dried beans, crusts or crumpled foil are placed inside so that the pastry keeps its shape. However, I find a better method with all pastry doughs is to invert the containers and cover them with dough. Except for large containers, foil is preferable to metal.

I also prefer to fashion each case from its individual piece of dough; this may not be quicker, but the pastry does not deteriorate from much handling, re-rolling and the addition of extra flour. Experience will soon indicate the amount of dough needed for each particular case. Roll this out on a piece of floured greaseproof paper, it will then be easier to handle. Invert the container to be covered on top of the dough and cut round the rim, leaving a margin of just over $\frac{1}{8}$ in ($\frac{1}{4}$ cm), wider, if the container is deep. Should you have the right sized pastry cutter, that's fine—otherwise use a knife.

To bake unfrozen Brush the outside of the container lightly with vegetable oil. This is not always necessary, certainly not with puff pastry, but is a wise precaution. Lay the shaped dough on the inverted container and mould it gently but firmly round the sides. Place on a cold baking sheet and bake in a preheated oven, set according to type of dough, for about 10 to 15 minutes, or until a nice pale brown. Place containers, pastry sides down, on a wire tray (not too large for the oven) and, after a few minutes, carefully lever the containers out of the pastry cases and, if necessary, return them (still on the tray) to the oven for a further few minutes to cook the insides.

To freeze The uncooked pastry for the cases can be frozen two ways: the rolled out pastry can either be moulded over oiled inverted foil containers, as already described, or packed flat in rounds of appropriate size in layers on a polystyrene tray (p. 19). The covered containers are stacked one on top of the other, separated by pieces of clinging film. The rounds of flat-shaped dough are separated by pieces of waxed paper. Both are packed in polythene bags and sealed before freezing.

To bake when frozen Shapes frozen over inverted containers are placed with their containers on a cold baking sheet. When the rounds are frozen flat, the inverted containers are placed on a cold baking sheet and the rounds placed centrally on top of them. In both cases put the baking sheets into a cold oven set at the correct temperature for the dough used. Bake for about 15 to 20 minutes. With flat shapes, investigate after 5–7 minutes and, if necessary, gently mould the newly thawed dough over the containers.

Orthodox Vol-au-Vent Cases *Oven setting 475° F—240° C—Mark 9*

Large cases, suitable for fish, poultry or meat fillings (pp. 101–4), need About 3½ oz (87·5 g) Puff Pastry Dough (p. 153) for each case and two pastry cutters, 4½ in (11 cm) and 3½ in (9 cm).

Smaller cases need About 2 oz (50 g) Puff Pastry Dough (for each case) and two pastry cutters, 3½ in (9 cm) and 2½ in (5 cm).

Miniature cases, just right for canapés and known as Bouchées, need

About ½ oz (12·5 g) Puff Pastry Dough (for each case) and two pastry cutters, 2 in (5 cm) and 1¼ in (3 cm).

Cut pieces of chilled dough of the correct weight. Roll these, keeping them as circular as possible, until they are slightly bigger than the larger of the two cutters. Trim the circles with the cutter. Using the smaller cutter, cut out the centres. Set aside the outer rings. Roll out the centre rounds again, keeping them as circular as possible, until they are a little bigger than the larger cutter—how much does not seem to matter, but to get a well-shaped case they must be definitely larger. Do not trim these rounds, just lay them on a cold baking sheet (if to be baked) or on a working surface (if to be frozen). Brush round the edges with a little cold water and fit the rings on the rounds, leaving a small surround of dough.
The vol-au-vents look attractive as they are, but if you would like a glaze, brush them with egg, egg and milk, or just milk.
(If lids are needed for the cases, these are easily made from the scraps of dough left after the first cut. Knead these together and mould into a rectangular slab. Then carry out 11 and 12, given for Puff Pastry on p. 155, several times. Finish with 11 and cut out small rounds.)

To bake unfrozen Place the still cold vol-au-vents and lids on the cold sheet into a preheated oven. Bake about 10 minutes, and a little longer, if necessary, at a lower temperature.

To freeze Pack the vol-au-vents and lids in layers on a polystyrene tray (p. 19), separating the layers with waxed paper. Pack in a polythene bag, seal and freeze.

To bake frozen Lay unthawed vol-au-vents on a cold baking sheet and place in a cold oven. Bake about 15 minutes or until cooked and well risen.

Square Vol-au-Vent Cases

These are a novelty, so easy to make and economical of freezer space.

Roll out pieces of dough into squares $\frac{1}{4}$ to $\frac{3}{8}$ in ($\frac{1}{2}$ to $\frac{3}{4}$ cm) thick, according to their size. Cut the edges to true up the sides. Cut out squares in the centres, leaving frames from $\frac{1}{4}$ to $\frac{3}{8}$ in ($\frac{1}{2}$ to $\frac{3}{4}$ cm) wide, again according to the size of the squares. Then continue as for the orthodox vol-au-vents.

Vol-au-Vent Flan Cases

These do look professional, and could not be simpler to make. Just follow the directions given for Vol-au-Vent Cases, but instead of cutters of different sizes, use plates, and cut round these with a knife. Experience will soon show you how much dough is needed for the plates you have chosen. A really large flan can be made using a bread board and a large meat plate or a sandwich tin. The sandwich tin is a good idea if the flan is to be served with a fruit and jelly filling (p. 132).

Puff Pastry Slices

These are the simplest of all Puff Dough products. Stored baked in a tin, or unbaked in the freezer, they can be used to make a variety of speedy yet attractive sweets (p. 124).
Cut off a rectangular piece of freshly made or newly thawed dough. Roll it to a thickness of $\frac{1}{4}$ to $\frac{3}{8}$ in ($\frac{1}{2}$ to $\frac{3}{4}$ cm), keeping it symmetrical. Cut a fraction off each of the sides and the resulting rectangle into oblongs or squares.

To bake unfrozen, To freeze and *To bake frozen* As given for Orthodox Vol-au-Vents (p. 159).

Savoury Sauces

Basic Rich White Sauce · Rich White Sauce with Vegetables · Basic Rich White Sauce Variations · Tomato Cream Sauce · Mustard Cream Sauce · Curry Cream Sauce · Cheese Cream Sauce · Cheese Foundation Sauce · Sauce Soubise · Onion and Tomato or Pimento Sauce · Curry

Sauce · Moly Sauce · Drawn Butter Sauce · Sweet Sour Sauce · Dutch Sauce · Canadian Mayonnaise · Sauce Espagnol · Italian Meat Sauce · French Dressing

Basic Rich White Sauce

This requires:

¼ lb (100 g) butter, or margarine
3 oz (75 g) plain flour
1 pint (500 ml) warm milk

Melt the butter or margarine in a saucepan. Remove from heat, and using a wooden spoon, gradually stir in the flour. Cook gently for a minute or so, then remove from heat. Gradually add the milk, stirring continuously. When quite smooth, return pan to heat, and stir until the mixture boils. Lower heat and cook for a few minutes, stirring occasionally.

To freeze Pour the sauce into suitable rectangular containers. Chill. The sauce will then be firm enough to mark into sections or small blocks with the back of a knife. (18 equal sections will each consist of about 1 heaped tablespoon (20 ml) sauce.) Block freeze (p. 16), but before packing the block in a polythene bag, cut it into the marked sections.

To use when frozen This thick buttery sauce can be used in the following recipes: Fish Cooked in Rich White Sauce (p. 50), Fish Cakes (p. 51), Fish Pie (p. 52) and Soups made from Frozen Sauces (p. 49).

Rich White Sauce with Vegetables

Basic Rich White Sauce is excellent with pressure-cooked vegetables or those boiled in very little water. While the vegetables are cooking, thaw the sauce in a heavy pan over gentle heat. Add enough of the vegetable liquid to make the sauce the required consistency. This should also provide all the necessary flavour and seasoning.

Basic Rich White Sauce Variations

A variety of sauces can be made by adding a selection of ingredients to Basic Rich White Sauce. The following are a few suggestions, and the given quantities are intended to be added to about 1 heaped tablespoon (20 ml) or 1½ oz (38 g) of the basic sauce.

Tomato Cream Sauce

To be served with fish, eggs, rice and pasta.
Additions to 1 heaped tablespoon (20 ml) Basic Rich White Sauce:

3 tablespoons (45 ml) milk
3 teaspoons (15 ml) tomato purée
1 teaspoon (5 ml) garlic vinegar
½–1 teaspoon (2·5–5 ml) sugar
salt and pepper to taste

Mustard Cream Sauce

To be served with grilled or fried herrings or mackerel, bacon, sausages, etc.
Additions to 1 heaped tablespoon (20 ml) Basic Rich White Sauce:

3 tablespoons (45 ml) milk
1½ teaspoons (7·5 ml) made mustard
salt and pepper to taste

Curry Cream Sauce

To be served over hard-boiled eggs, fish, potatoes, etc.
Additions to 1 heaped tablespoon (20 ml) Basic Rich White Sauce:

3 tablespoons (45 ml) milk
2 teaspoons (10 ml) curry powder
½–1 teaspoon (2·5–5 ml) black treacle

a good pinch of garlic salt
salt to taste
¼ teaspoon (1·25 ml) lemon juice

Cheese Cream Sauce

To be served over broccoli, cauliflower, boiled celery, leeks, poached eggs, etc.
Additions to 1 heaped tablespoon (20 ml) Basic Rich White Sauce:

2 tablespoons (30 ml) vegetable stock, or milk
1 oz (25 g) grated cheese
salt and pepper to taste

Cheese Foundation Sauce

A good and useful sauce, when Cheese Foundation (p. 86) is available. To each tablespoon (15 ml) Cheese Foundation add:

1 teaspoon (5 ml) milk, or beer

Place over gentle heat and stir with a wooden spoon until hot and completely blended.

Sauce Soubise (a French Onion Sauce)

Allow:

2 large, 3 medium, or 4 small onions
½ pint (250 ml) water
1 tablespoon (15 ml) flour
8 fluid oz (200 ml) milk
salt, pepper and nutmeg to taste
2½ oz (62·5 g) butter

Gently boil the onions until the water has almost evaporated and they are very soft. Chop them up with kitchen scissors, while still in the pan. Sprinkle in the flour and add the milk. Stir over gentle heat until the sauce thickens, then simmer for 5 minutes. Add seasoning to taste and the butter. Liquidize the sauce or pass it through a moulin-légumes or a sieve.

To freeze Pour sauce into suitable rectangular containers, chill and block freeze (p. 16).

To use Sauce Soubise is good served with fish (Fish Soubise, pp. 49–50), with eggs (Eggs Soubise, p. 84), and as a base for soups (Soups made from Frozen Sauces, p. 49).

Onion and Tomato or Pimento Sauce

Allow:

½ lb (200 g) onions, sliced
1½ oz (37·5 g) vegetable margarine
14 oz (350 g) tin tomatoes, or pimentos (sweet red peppers)
¼ teaspoon (1·25 ml) salt
2 teaspoons (10 ml) sugar (with tomato)
¼ teaspoon (1·25 ml) pepper
2 teaspoons (10 ml) lemon juice
a little parsley, thyme and marjoram (fresh if possible)

Fry the onion in a covered pan until it is clear. Add the remaining ingredients and either liquidize the mixture or put it through a moulin-légumes or a nylon sieve.

To freeze Pour the sauce into suitable rectangular containers. Chill and block freeze, dividing the partially frozen sauce into sections (p. 16).

To use Onion and Tomato Sauce can be used in many ways, and the following are only a few suggestions: with fish, sausages, liver and bacon, as an ingredient in soups (p. 49), casseroles, savouries.

Curry Sauce

Allow:

- 1½ oz (37·5 g) butter, or margarine
- 2 onions, sliced
- 1 large cooking apple, peeled, cored and chopped
- 1 teaspoon (5 ml) black treacle
- 1 tablespoon (15 ml) marmalade
- 2–4 teaspoons (10–20 ml) curry powder, according to taste and strength of powder
- 1 tablespoon (15 ml) flour
- ½ teaspoon (2·5 ml) salt
- ½ pint (250 ml) milk
- ½ pint (250 ml) water

Melt butter in a pan over medium heat and cook the onion and apple (pan covered) until the apple is mushy. Remove from heat. Add the treacle, marmalade, curry powder, flour and salt. Mix well with a wooden spoon. Replace over heat and cook for a few minutes, stirring continuously. Gradually add the liquids. Increase heat and, still stirring, cook until the sauce thickens.
The sauce can be left as it is or liquidized or passed through a plastic sieve or a moulin-légumes.

To freeze Pour sauce into suitable rectangular containers. Chill and block freeze (p. 16).

To use Curry Sauce can be used in many ways, including the following suggestions: in Curried Chicken (p. 81), in Curried Eggs (p. 84), in Soups made from Frozen Sauces (p. 49).

Moly Sauce

Allow:

- ½ pint (250 ml) milk
- 6 cloves
- 3 in (7 cm) cinnamon stick

a little lemon grass, if available
4 oz (100 g) butter, or margarine
2 onions, sliced
2 tablespoons (30 ml) flour
2 teaspoons (10 ml) curry powder
pinch of salt
½ teaspoon (2·5 ml) saffron

Put the milk, spices and lemon grass in a pan and bring slowly to the boil. Reduce heat, draw pan slightly aside and leave for 10 minutes. In the meantime melt the fat in a second pan and fry the onion until soft but not brown. Remove from heat and stir in the flour, curry powder, salt and saffron. Cook the mixture for 2 minutes. When the spices have been sufficiently infused, gradually strain the flavoured milk into the roux and stir until the sauce thickens.

To freeze Pour the sauce into suitable rectangular containers. Chill and block freeze (p. 16).

To use This is a mild curry sauce from the Far East, used for Fish Moly (pp. 49–50) and a delicately flavoured Egg Curry (p. 84). Anyone with frozen blocks of this sauce is sure to find plenty more ways of appreciating it.

Drawn Butter Sauce

A nice, buttery, lemon-flavoured sauce.

Allow:

1 oz (25 g) butter, or margarine
2 rounded tablespoons (30 ml) plain flour
8 fluid oz (200 ml) stock or water and stock powder
salt and pepper to taste
1 extra oz (25 g) butter, or margarine, cut into four pieces
1 teaspoon (5 ml) lemon juice, fresh or bottled

Heat 1 oz (25 g) of fat, stir in the flour and cook gently for 2 minutes. Remove from heat and gradually stir in the liquid. Return to raised heat and continue to stir until the sauce thickens. Add seasoning. Then, leaving the pan over the heat, vigorously stir in a quarter of the remaining fat together with a quarter of the lemon juice until it is absorbed. Repeat three times.

To freeze Pour the sauce into suitable rectangular containers. Chill and block freeze (p. 16).

To use Serve with vegetables or fish (the sauce can be diluted with a chosen liquid).

Sweet Sour Sauce

This sauce is good served with pork or ham, also for reheating slices of roast pork.

Allow:

3 dessertspoons (30 ml) dark brown sugar
1 dessertspoon (10 ml) cornflour
1 dessertspoon (10 ml) soy sauce
4 dessertspoons (40 ml) vinegar
1 dessertspoon (10 ml) tomato purée
salt to taste
½ pint (250 ml) water
2–3 oz (50–75 g) finely chopped mustard pickle, or fresh pineapple
1 oz (25 g) finely chopped pickled onion, or grated raw onion

Mix the sugar and cornflour in a small saucepan. Stir in the soy sauce and vinegar, and when a smooth paste, mix in the tomato purée. Then gradually stir in the water and add the salt. Place pan over moderate heat and stir until the sauce thickens. Add the remaining ingredients and cook for a further minute.

To freeze Pour the sauce into suitable rectangular containers. Chill and block freeze (p. 16).

To use See Left-over Roast Meat (p. 182).

Dutch Sauce

This unusual version of Sauce Hollandaise is an old German recipe. It is carefree, freezes well and reheats without trouble, provided it is not allowed to boil.

3 oz (75 g) butter, or vegetable margarine
1 heaped tablespoon (20 ml) plain flour
½ pint (250 ml) stock, or water and stock powder
4 or 5 egg yolks
1 tablespoon (15 ml) lemon juice
salt to taste

Heat 1 oz (25 g) of the fat in a pan—preferably the top of a double saucepan. Stir in the flour and cook until it becomes a delicate golden colour. Add the stock and continue to stir until the mixture boils. Remove from heat and, with no double saucepan, transfer the sauce to a basin that fits over a pan. Beat up the yolks with the lemon juice and add to the cooled stock. Season. Place pan or basin over boiling water and stir well until the sauce begins to thicken. Then add the remaining 2 oz (50 g) fat, cut into small pieces, and stir until the sauce is quite thick. It must not be allowed to boil.

To freeze Pour sauce into suitable rectangular containers. Chill and block freeze (p. 16).

To use Serve with vegetables or fish or use in Fish Hollandaise (pp. 49–51).

Canadian Mayonnaise

This easy to make mayonnaise is not as rich as orthodox mayonnaise and has the advantage of not objecting to slow cooking or freezing.

2 egg yolks
1 teaspoon (5 ml) each salt and dry mustard
¼ teaspoon (1·25 ml) pepper

1 tablespoon (15 ml) sugar (optional)
4 fluid oz (100 ml) olive oil
4 fluid oz (100 ml) vinegar, or lemon juice (fresh or bottled)
1 oz (25 g) margarine
2½ tablespoons (37·5 ml) plain flour
8 fluid oz (200 ml) warm water

Put the yolks, seasonings, sugar, oil, vinegar or lemon in a mixing bowl. Melt the margarine in a saucepan. Stir in the flour, and when smooth, gradually add the water. Place over medium heat, and stir until the mixture thickens and boils. Immediately pour the hot sauce over the other ingredients and whisk the lot together like mad with a rotary whisk. In a matter of moments a lovely creamy mayonnaise is produced. When cold, either pour into a jar (it keeps well for months in a refrigerator), or it can be block frozen (p. 16) or used in Fish Mayonnaise (pp. 49–51).

Sauce Espagnol

This famous sauce, so often featured in haute cuisine, probably originated in Spain, but has been adopted by France for centuries. Now when a recipe demands Sauce Espagnol, perhaps only a little, we, with our small freezers, can produce it with smug satisfaction, for instance for Lambs' Kidneys à la Señorita (p. 77).
To prepare 1 pint (500 ml) allow:

2 oz (50 g) butter
2 oz (50 g) carrots, diced
2 oz (50 g) onions, diced
2 tablespoons (37·5 ml) flour
2½ fluid oz (62·5 ml) white wine, or dry cider
a bouquet garni
1½ tablespoons (22·5 ml) tomato purée
1 oz (25 g) mushroom stalks
1½ pints (750 ml) stock, or water and stock cube
1 tablespoon (15 ml) sherry

Melt the butter in a large pan and add the diced vegetables. Simmer gently until the vegetables are slightly coloured. Add the flour, mix well with a wooden spoon and cook gently until the flour begins to brown. Then very gradually add the stock and the wine or cider. Bring to the boil before adding the bouquet garni, tomato purée and mushroom stalks. Simmer gently for an hour, skimming the surface carefully as the scum rises.

Strain the sauce through a sieve into another saucepan. Bring to the boil again and skim if necessary. Add the sherry. Now measure the sauce. If over 1 pint (500 ml), reduce by a little further boiling: if under 1 pint, mix sufficient boiling water with the strained vegetables and strain the resulting liquid into the sauce.

To freeze Chill and block freeze (p. 16) into ¼ pint (125 ml) blocks.

Italian Meat Sauce

With blocks of this sauce in the freezer, dishes like Spaghetti Bolognese (p. 99) or Lasagne (p. 100) can be served quickly and easily.

Ingredients:

1 onion 1 carrot 1 stick of celery 1 clove garlic (optional) 5 oz (125 g) bacon (optional)	minced or finely chopped

2 tablespoons (30 ml) olive oil
½ lb (200 g) lean minced beef, pork, or veal
1 small tin of tomatoes
1 tablespoon (15 ml) tomato purée
¼ teaspoon (1·25 ml) each, dried basil, thyme and marjoram
½ teaspoon (2·5 ml) salt
1½ teaspoons (7·5 ml) sugar
2½ fluid oz (62·5 ml) wine (red or white), or stock

Gently fry the onion, carrot, celery, garlic and bacon in the oil for about 5 minutes in a covered pan. Add the meat and continue to cook, still gently, and stirring occasionally, for a further 10 minutes.

Add the tin of tomatoes (having first cut up the tomatoes), the purée, herbs, salt and sugar. Blend well before stirring the liquid into the mixture. Cover and cook very gently for 40 minutes, adding a little more liquid if necessary.

To freeze Pour sauce into suitable rectangular containers, chill and block freeze (p. 16).

To use from freezer Thaw blocks in a heavy pan over gentle heat, stirring occasionally.

French Dressing

This classic dressing is used for tossed green salads which, of course, cannot be frozen, and also for cooked vegetable salads and hors d'oeuvres, which can be stored in the freezer, e.g. Celeriac and Beetroot Salads (pp. 120–1).
Make the dressing in a pint screw-topped jar. It keeps for months in the fridge or a cool cupboard.

Pour into the jar:

- 6 fluid oz (150 ml) salad oil
- 2 fluid oz (50 ml) vinegar, or lemon juice (fresh or bottled)
- 1–3 teaspoons (5–15 ml) sugar
- 1 clove garlic, cut in half
- 1 teaspoon (5 ml) Worcester Sauce (optional)
- ½–1 teaspoon (2·5–5 ml) salt
- ½ teaspoon (2·5 ml) paprika (optional)
- ¼ teaspoon (1·25 ml) freshly ground pepper

Before using, shake jar until all the ingredients are well blended.

Cream and Custard

Dairy Cream · Home-made Cream · Home-made Single Cream · Sour Cream · Custard · Custard Cream

Dairy Cream

To find fresh cream in the fridge whenever this is wanted is, of course, the ideal, but difficult to realize. The next best is a constant, if small, supply of cream in the freezer.

If possible, freeze pasteurized cream with 40 per cent butterfat, i.e. double cream or clotted cream (when you can get it). Should a lighter whipping cream or single cream be wanted, top of the milk can be stirred into thawed double cream. Cream with under 40 per cent butterfat can be frozen. It is apt to separate when thawed, but this is not disastrous, since a little whisking will soon rectify the trouble.

The pundits disagree widely over the storage time for frozen cream. I prefer not to keep mine in the freezer longer than 2 months and get the best results when the double cream is whipped before freezing. If liked, a little sugar can be added.

To freeze Turn the cream into a rectangular plastic container and block freeze (p. 16).

To use from freezer See p. 32.

Home-made Cream (made in a liquidizer or manual cream-maker)

A delicious double cream, comparable to dairy cream, can easily be made if, each time a bottle of full cream milk is broached, 1–2 in (3–5 cm) of the top of the milk is poured into a small rectangular plastic container kept for that purpose in the fridge frozen food compartment or, in the case of fridge-freezers, the freezer.

When at least ¼ pint (125 ml) top of the milk has been collected, eject the frozen block into a saucepan over gentle heat. As soon as thawed, pour the liquid into a measure. Return this to the pan with:

salt-free butter, cut into pieces, in the ratio of 1½–2 oz (37·5–50 g) to ¼ pint (125 ml) top of the milk

Raise heat and bring the mixture to the boil. While still hot,

liquidize—not more than 30 seconds—or pump the mixture through a cream-maker. Cool and chill as quickly as possible. After about 12 hours, the thick crust that will have formed on top must be stirred into the thinner cream below.
The cream can now be whipped up and either served, made into Ice Cream (pp. 126–7), or, if not wanted for a day or two, frozen, according to directions given for Dairy Cream (p. 172).

Home-made Single Cream

This is useful, both for economy or when single dairy cream or top of the milk are not available. It can be frozen, but when thawed may separate, in which case give it a light whisk. Allow:

2½ oz (67·5 g) butter (salted or salt-free, according to savoury or sweet use of cream) to ¼ pint (125 ml) milk

Boil up the milk and butter and either liquidize or pump through a cream-making machine.

Sour Cream

Sour Cream can be made quickly with whipping or single cream, dairy or home-made, provided they are icy cold.

For a small quantity Add ¼ teaspoon (1·25 ml) lemon juice (bottled or fresh) to 1 tablespoon (15 ml) cream.

For a larger quantity Add 1 dessertspoon (10 ml) lemon juice to ¼ pint (125 ml) cream.

An easy but slower method is to let the cream stand in a warm place until it has soured.

Custard

Soft egg custard behaves like single cream. It can be frozen satisfactorily but, when thawed, it will separate and must be lightly whipped before serving.

Custard Cream

Custard Cream, on the other hand, freezes and thaws well. It is delicious with fruit and perfect for trifles. With a liquidizer it can be made with milk and salt-free butter, otherwise single cream is used.

Method 1 (made with a liquidizer)

3 oz (75 g) salt-free butter, melted
7 fluid oz (175 ml) milk
1½ oz (37·5 ml) caster sugar
½–1 teaspoon (2·5–5 ml) vanilla sugar
3 egg yolks

Liquidize the melted butter, milk, sugar and vanilla sugar for 10 seconds. Add the yolks and liquidize a further 3 seconds. Pour the mixture either into the top of a double saucepan or into a basin that fits over a saucepan. Cook over boiling water, and stir with a wooden spoon until the custard thickens and coats the spoon well.

To freeze Pour the custard into rectangular plastic containers. Chill and block freeze (p. 16).

To use from freezer As given for frozen Cream on p. 32.

Method 2

½ pint (250 ml) single cream
3 egg yolks
1½ oz (37·5 g) caster sugar
½– 1 teaspoon (2·5–5 ml) vanilla sugar

Pour the cream either into the top of a double saucepan or into a basin that fits over a saucepan. Heat over boiling water.
In another basin beat together the yolks and sugar and gradually add first the warm cream, then the vanilla sugar. Pour the mixture back into the saucepan or basin over boiling water, and stir with a wooden spoon until the custard thickens and coats the spoon well.

To freeze and *To use from freezer* As given for Method 1.

Yeast Cookery

The Yeast · Risen White Dough · French Loaf · Bread Rolls · Bread Sticks · Croissants · Chelsea Buns · Pizzas

Very small freezers obviously can accommodate only the odd loaf of bread or several rolls or croissants. Yet when your freezer houses a few blocks of Risen White Dough, you can enjoy easy, quick but varied yeast cookery.

The Yeast

Before I owned a freezer, when yeast had to be used within a few days of its purchase, I was often obliged to make use of dried yeast —hopefully presuming it was equally efficient, which it certainly is not. Now, with a freezer, fresh yeast is always available. How long frozen yeast keeps its quality I don't know. A small amount that had been overlooked for quite six months, proved entirely satisfactory.

Buy ¼ or ½ lb (100 or 200 g) fresh yeast. Divide it into 2 oz (50 g) portions. Wrap these individually in a clinging film before packing them in a polythene bag. Seal and freeze.

To use Thaw at room temperature about 60 minutes or, if wanted in a hurry, frozen yeast can be grated.

Risen White Dough

- 1½ teaspoons (7·5 ml) sugar
- ½ pint (250 ml) half milk, half water, lukewarm
- 1 teaspoon (5 ml) flour
- 2 oz (50 g)* fresh yeast
- 1½ lb (600 g) strong white flour

* Dough to be frozen requires twice as much yeast as normally used.

1 teaspoon (5 ml) salt
1½ oz (37·5 g) butter
1 egg beaten into ¼ pint (125 ml) milk

In a small basin, dissolve the sugar in the milk and water. Sprinkle on to it the teaspoonful of flour and crumble in the yeast. Cover and leave for about 10 minutes or until frothy.
In the meantime, sieve the flour and salt into a large mixing bowl. Rub in the butter and mix in the frothy yeast mixture, the egg and milk. Work to a firm dough which leaves the bowl clean. Knead this dough on an unfloured working surface for about 5 minutes. Place in a large oiled plastic bag, fasten and leave in the fridge to rise for about 2 hours. Knead or 'knock back' this risen dough as quickly as possible. Divide it into four portions, pack in individual bags, seal and freeze. With experience you may prefer to divide the dough into definite amounts for particular uses.

To use from freezer Thaw in the fridge overnight or at room temperature for 2–3 hours. Knead, shape, prove and bake according to recipe.
This is slightly richer than the usual white loaf dough, but is excellent for the following recipes.

French Loaf *Oven setting 400° F—200° C—Mark 6*

Shape the thawed, 'knocked back' Risen White Dough (p. 175) into a long roll or a plait. To make a plait: divide the roll into three and roll each piece into a long sausage. Dampen the ends and secure the three at one end. Plait loosely and secure the other end. Place on a lightly greased floured baking sheet, inside a large oiled polythene bag, and leave in a warm place to double its size. Brush loaf with beaten egg; if liked, sprinkle with poppy seeds. Bake about 20 minutes in preheated oven.

Bread Rolls *Oven setting 400° F—200° C—Mark 6*

To make 4–5 rolls allow ½ lb (200 g) Risen White Dough (p. 175).

Knead the newly thawed dough and cut it into 4 or 5 pieces. Knead each piece again before shaping it as follows.

Dinner or breakfast rolls Using the palm of the hand, roll into balls.

Cottage rolls Cut one-third off each piece of dough. Roll the larger and smaller pieces into balls. Put the smaller on top of the larger, moistening where they join. With a floured finger, make a hole right through the centre of each roll.

Plaits As given for French Loaf (p. 176).

Knots Make 9 in (23 cm) to 10 in (25 cm) long rolls and tie into loose knots.

Winkles Form into rolls as for Knots. Anchor one end to the working surface and wind the roll into a shell-like coil.

Place the shaped rolls on a lightly greased, floured baking sheet inside a large oiled polythene bag and leave in a warm place to double in size. Brush with milk or beaten egg or, if a soft top is preferred, fat or cooking oil. Bake in preheated oven for about 15 minutes.

Bread Sticks *Oven setting 350° F—180° C—Mark 4*

It is good to have these on tap for guests. They store quite well in tins, but, as they take up little storage space, are better frozen if they are to be kept for some time. Unless Bread Sticks are wanted in quantity, it is more practical to make them when more Risen White Dough (p. 175) has been thawed than is actually needed.
Roll the kneaded dough into sticks about 8 in (20 cm) long and as thick as your little finger. Prove for about 20 minutes on a lightly floured and greased baking sheet. Brush with milk and sprinkle with sea salt. Bake in preheated oven until a light brown. To crispen the sticks, either bake them a further 20 minutes in a much cooler oven, or leave them in the oven with the door ajar and the heat turned off.

Croissants *Oven setting 425° F—220° C—Mark 7*

To make 6 croissants allow:

½ lb (200 g) just thawed Risen White Dough* (p. 175)
2 oz (50 g) hard margarine, chilled*

1. Roll the dough into a rectangle about 11 × 5 in (27 × 12 cm).
2. Cover the top two-thirds of the dough with half the margarine cut into small dabs.
3. Fold the uncovered dough over half the margarine-covered dough.
4. Fold again to cover the remaining dough and margarine. Press the open edges with the rolling pin to seal them.
5. Turn the block to leave the closed side on the right, and roll this again into an 11 × 5 in (27 × 12 cm) rectangle.

Repeat 2–5 once. Then fold as before, roll into the same-sized rectangle and fold again into a block. Repeat once again.
Roll this block into a circle about ⅛ in (¼ cm) thick and 12 in (30 cm) in diameter. Cut the circle into 6 equal segments. Moisten the tops of these triangular wedges and, starting at the bases, roll them up and fasten with the dampened tops. Shape into crescents. Place the croissants on to a dampened baking sheet, the sealed tops underneath. Leave to relax at room temperature for about 30 minutes. Brush with beaten egg and bake in preheated oven 15–20 minutes. Croissants are delicious freshly baked, but keep well for a day or so and can be reheated in the oven, under a slow grill, or in a thick pan with a well-fitting lid over gentle heat. Of course, if you have room for them, you can freeze a few for a later date.

* Provided both the dough and margarine are icy cold, I find that the croissants can be shaped without being rested and chilled during the process.

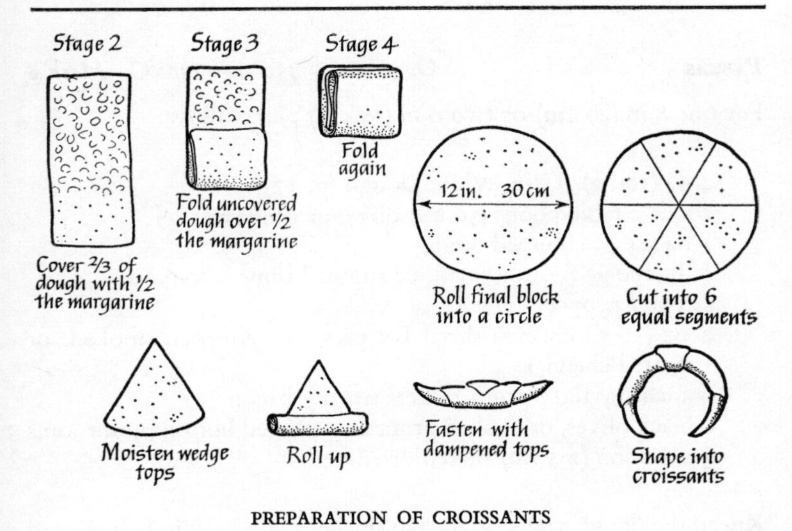

PREPARATION OF CROISSANTS

Chelsea Buns *Oven setting 375° F—190° C—Mark 5*

To make 7–8 buns allow:

12 oz (300 g) Risen White Dough (p. 175)
1½ oz (37·5 g) warmed lard
6 oz (150 g) mixed dried fruit
¾ teaspoon (3·75 ml) mixed spice
2 oz (50 g) sugar

Roll the dough to an oblong 12 in (30 cm) long and ¼ in (½ cm) thick. Blend together the remaining ingredients and spread the mixture evenly over the dough, pressing it in with a palette knife. Roll up tightly, swiss roll fashion. With a sharp knife cut into slices ¾–1 in (2–2·5 cm) thick. Place these, cut side down, fairly close together, in an oblong or square lightly greased baking tin in a large polythene bag and leave until the buns are puffy. Bake towards the top of a preheated oven for about 20 minutes.

When cooked, either dredge with sugar or cover with a thin lemon-flavoured water icing.

Pizzas *Oven setting 450° F—230° C—Mark 8*

For one 8 in (20 cm) or two 6 in (15 cm) pizzas allow:

4 oz (100 g) Risen White Dough (p. 175)
about 2 tablespoons (30 ml) olive, or sunflower oil
1 oz (25 g) chopped onion
½ lb (200 g) fresh skinned, or strained tinned, tomatoes
salt and pepper
2 oz (50 g) cheese—sliced bel paese, or Austrian smoked, or grated cheddar
6 anchovy fillets; or 3 rashers streaky bacon
6 black olives, or cooked prunes, or cooked button mushrooms
½ teaspoon (2·5 ml) mixed dried herbs

Knead the dough well and for the smaller pizzas, cut in half. Knead again into one or two balls. Press or roll these into rounds and fit snugly into 8 in (20 cm) or 6 in (15 cm) lightly greased sandwich or flan tins with loose bottoms or flan rings on a lightly greased baking sheet. Brush the dough surface with a little oil.

Fry the onions in oil until transparent and spread over the oiled dough. Cover to within ½ in (1 cm) of the edges with sliced tomato. Season well with salt and pepper. Put a layer of sliced or grated cheese over the tomatoes. Decorate with thin strips of anchovy fillets or bacon—the bacon strips twisted like barley sugar. Arrange these like the spokes of a wheel and place stoned and halved olives or prunes or mushrooms between the spokes. Sprinkle the herbs and a little more oil over the pizza. Leave in a warm place for 20–30 minutes to prove.

Bake about 20 minutes in preheated oven.

To freeze Chill rapidly. If the pizzas are wanted in the near future and freezer space allows, pack uncut in polythene bags; otherwise cut into wedges, wrap these in clinging film and pack in bags, alternating wedge tips and bases. Seal and freeze.

To serve from freezer If time allows, thaw at room temperature for about 2 hours before heating in a hot oven. Otherwise place frozen in the hot oven. Whole pizzas will need about 30 minutes—wedges about 20 minutes.

Freezing Surplus Foods

We cannot store a great number of these foods in our small freezers —yet if, whenever practical, these odds and ends are frozen, it is surprising just how many can be housed and how valuable they may be.

Partly Used Tins

These are a good example. The contents can be block frozen in those small rectangular margarine containers or in the case of tomato purée or very small quantities of liquid, in ice-cube trays. You may like to freeze the purée in teaspoons (5 ml).

Eggs

These can be frozen satisfactorily in the freezer or in the fridge storage compartment and kept in the latter for a month. Whole eggs are only likely to be left after beaten egg has been used for crumbing or glazing. There won't be much, but this can be frozen in ice-cube containers and is well worth saving for another day.

Egg Yolks

Unless a little salt or sugar is mixed with the yolk before freezing, it may become thick and gummy. Allow to each yolk either just under ¼ teaspoon (1·25 ml) salt, or just under ½ teaspoon (2·5 ml) sugar.

Mark the frozen blocks, giving the number of yolks and whether salty or sweet. As a rough guide 1 tablespoon (15 ml) thawed yolk = 1 egg yolk. Thaw yolks either in the fridge or at room temperature, or, if in a hurry, like Cream (p. 32).

Egg Whites

These do not require the addition of salt or sugar before freezing. Mark the frozen blocks with the number of whites contained. Approximately 2 tablespoons (30 ml) thawed white = 1 egg white. Thaw as given for egg yolks. Frozen whites whip very well, even better than unfrozen.

Left-over Roast Meat

Cut the cold meat into slices. Wrap them in clinging film, pack in a polythene bag, seal and freeze.

To use from freezer Cut the frozen slices into strips. Place them in a saucepan over gentle heat with an appropriate freshly made or frozen sauce. Roast pork in Sweet Sour Sauce (p. 167) served really hot with boiled rice or noodles is particularly good.

Left-over Cooked Bacon

If this is not crisp, should be crispened. It should then be crumbled up and frozen. It can be used in casseroles or as a garnish for potatoes or any savoury dish.

Left-over Cooked Ham

Before freezing, finely mince the ham and mix it with a little butter. It can be served as a spread or used in savoury dishes.

Left-overs in Soups (see p 48)

Left-overs in General (see p 30)

Store-cupboard Supplements

Perhaps the greatest joy a freezer provides is the knowledge that for most occasions, whatever the time, a good suitable meal can easily be provided. Of course we with our small freezers have our limitations, but a well-stocked supplementary store-cupboard can stretch those limits. Here are some ways of filling it. Be sure to freeze the unused contents of opened tins as soon as possible.

Tinned Cream Soups

These can be served as a first course, used to stretch a frozen soup, or be part of a Store-cupboard Filling (p. 104) for frozen Pastry Cases or Pancakes (pp. 157 and 97).

Tins of Salmon, Tuna Fish, Sardines, Crab, Lobster, Shrimps, Prawns

Any of these can be served with thawed Vegetable Salad (p. 120) as an hors d'oeuvre, or they can be used in a Store-cupboard Filling (p. 104) for frozen Pastry Cases or Pancakes (pp. 157 and 97).

Tinned Cocktail Sausages

Can be served in Miniature Pancakes (p. 98) with drinks, or with a thawed Vegetable Salad (p. 120) as an hors d'oeuvre.

Tinned Meats with Sauce or Gravy

These are useful for augmenting suitable casseroled dishes during the heating process. The tins can also be used to fill Vol-au-Vents or Pancakes (pp. 158 and 97).

Tinned Beans

These can be mixed with thawing Chilli-Con-Carne (p. 61), and used to stretch inadequate casseroles or served as an hors d'oeuvre with thawed Vegetable Salad (p. 120).

Tinned or Vacuum Packed New Potatoes

These are delicious and useful. They can be served hot with a little parsley and butter or cold with French Dressing (p. 171) etc., as a potato salad.

Vacuum Packed Vegetables

If you happen to be out of frozen vegetables, these are, in my opinion, preferable to either tinned or quick-dried dehydrated vegetables.

Tinned Creamed Mushrooms

These can be added to a variety of thawing dishes, used to fill Pancakes (p. 97) or in a Store-cupboard Filling (p. 104).

Tins or Bottles of Pimentos (Sweet Red Peppers) Pitted Black and Green Olives, Cocktail Onions, Anchovies

These will all come in handy for garnishes.

Sponge Cakes

Superb trifles can always be made whenever there are sponge cakes, jam, sherry and garnishes in the cupboard and Custard Cream (p. 174) and cream in the freezer.

Crystallized Fruits, Glacé Cherries, Angelica, Preserved or Crystallized Ginger, Split Almonds, Dried Walnuts

Any of these will add the finishing touch to frozen or unfrozen desserts.

Index

Almond Biscuits, 142
Artichokes, blanching and freezing, 107
Asparagus, blanching and freezing, 107
Aubergines, blanching and freezing, 107

Bacon
  cooked left-over, 182
  and Liver Filling, 103
  and Onion Roll, 90
  Potato Cakes, 89, 90
  storage time, 23
Bags, polythene, 18
Banana, 24
  and Fruit Sauce Pancakes, 125
  Splits, 129
Barbecued Spare Rib, 71
Beans, broad, runner and French, blanching and freezing, 107
Beef
  Boeuf Bourgignonne, 57
  Chilli-con-Carne, 61
  Flemish Braised Steak, 55
  freezing, 27
  Gobbets, 59
  Hamburgers, 62
  Hungarian Goulash, 58
  Mince Minute Steaks, 60
  Minute Steaks, 60
  roast, left-over, 182
  Smothered Steak, 56
  storage times, 23
  Swedish Meat Balls, 63
  thawing, 34–5
  and Vegetables, Simmered, 54
Beetroot
  Harvard, 114
  Salad, 120
Biscuits, using Cake Foundation, 142–6
  Almond, 142
  Cheese Nibbles, 146
  Continental Sugar, 144
  Ginger Snaps, 144–5
  Great-Grandmother's Chocolate, 143
  Peanut Nibbles, 145
  Shortcrust, 144
  Shrewsbury, 143
  Vienna, 143
Block Freezing, 16–17, 20
Boeuf Bourgignonne, 57
Boxes, plastic, for stacking, 21
Bread
  Croissants, 178–9
  freezing, 28
  French Loaf, 176
  Risen White Dough, 175–6
  Rolls, 176–7
  Sticks, 40, 177
  storage times, 23
  thawing, 31
Breadcrumbs, fresh, 29–30
Bredee (lamb stew), 65
Broccoli, blanching and freezing, 107
Brussels sprouts, blanching and freezing, 107
Buck Rarebit, 87
Buns
  Chelsea, 179
  Fruit, 137
Butter
  storage time, 23
  thawing, 31
Butterscotch
  Crunch Fillings, 133

Butterscotch—*cont.*
Nut Filling, 132
Sauce, 129
Sponge Pudding, 146–7

Cabbage, Sweet and Sour, 110
Cake Foundation, 133–6
Biscuits, cocktail, 145–6
Biscuits, sweet, 142–5
Cherry Cake, Rich, 141
Cherry Cakes, 138
Chocolate Cakes, 137
Fruit Buns, 137
Fruit Cake, Rich, 141
Fruit Cakes, 138
Lemon Curd, Mock, 151
Madeira Cake, 139
Orange Cake, 139
Orange Cakes, 137
Pain de Gênes, 139
Pastry, 150–1
Puddings and Sweets, 146–50
Queen Cakes, 138
Rice Cakes, 138
Scones, 141–2
Standard Sponge, 136
Sultana Cake, 140
Treacle Fruit Cake, 140
Victoria Sandwich, 135
Cakes *see also* Cake Foundation
freezing, 28
storage times, 23
thawing, 31–2
Carrots
blanching and freezing, 107
Buttered, 113
sliced, freezing, 29–30, 107
Cauliflower, blanching and freezing, 107
Celeriac, 112
Buttered, 113
Purée, 113
Salad, 121
in Sauce, 112
Celery
blanching and freezing, 107
à l'Italien, 111
Rarebit, 87
Sticks, 29–30, 107
Cheese *see also* Cheese Foundation
Aigrettes, 85
Bacon Potato Cakes, 90
Cream Sauce, 163
grated, 30
Nibbles, 146
storage time, 23
thawing, 32
Cheese Foundation, 86
Buck Rarebit, 87
Celery Rarebit, 87
Croque Monsieur, 88
Eggs, 88
Omelette, 88
Pancakes, 87
in Sandwiches, 89
Sauce, 163
in Soup, 49
Welsh Rarebit, 87
Chelsea Buns, 179
Cherry Cake, Rich, 141
Cherry Cakes, Small, 138
Chicken
Curried, 81
freezing, 27
Fried à l'Espagnol, 79
Marengo, 80
and Rice, 78
storage times, 23
thawing, 36
Chicken Liver
Filling, 104
Pilaff, 99
Rice Soufflé, 99
Chilli-con-Carne, 61
Chinese Sliced Pork, 70
Chocolate
Biscuits, Great-Grandmother's, 143
Butterscotch Sauce, 130

Chocolate—*cont.*
Cakes, 137
Sponge Pudding, 146–7
Cloves, 24
Cocktail biscuits, 145–6
Cod à la Norge, Baked, 53
Coffee beans, 29
Containers, freezer, 15, 16, 18, 19
Cooking frozen foods, 30–8
Copenhagen Fruit Pie, 150
Corn-on-the-Cob
blanching and freezing, 107
thawing, 37–8
Cornish Pasties, 95–6
Courgettes
blanching and freezing, 107
Casserole, 115
Cream, 171–4
Custard, 174
dairy, 172
freezing, 29, 172
home-made, 172
single, 24, 173
sour, 24, 173
storage time, 23
thawing, 32
Crêpes Suzette, 125
Croissants, 178–9
Croque Monsieur, 88
Cucumber, 24
Curried
Chicken, 81
Eggs, 84
Curry
Cream Sauce, 162
Puffs, 95–6
Sauce, 165
Custard, 173
Cream (1 and 2), 124, 174
pies, 24

Defrosting
involuntary, 25–6
voluntary, 24–5

Drawn Butter Sauce, 166
Dutch Sauce, 168

Eggs
and Celery à l'Italien, 111
Cheese, 88
Curried, 84
freezing, 181
hard-boiled, 24
Omelettes, Savoury, 84
Soubise, 84
storage time, 23
whites of, 182
yolks of, 181–2
Espagnol Sauce, 169

Fillings
Savoury, 101–4
Sweet, 129–33
Films, wrapping, 18
Fish
Baked Cod à la Norge, 53
Cakes, 51
Cooked in Sauce, 49–51
freezing, 27
Haddock Filling, 102
Kedgeree, 52
Pie, 52
storage time, 23
thawing, 32–3
Flaky Pastry, 156
Flan Cases, 157–60
Flemish Braised Steak, 55
Foil containers, 18, 20
Freezers, small, 13–14, 26–30
Freezing, 15–21
block, 16–17
foods not suitable, 24
open, 15, 19, 21
packaging for, 17–21
packing containers and materials, 16–19
surplus foods, 181

French
  Dressing, 171
  Loaf, 176
Fridge-freezers, 14
Fruit, 122–3
  Buns, 137
  Cake, Rich, 141
  Cakes, Small, 138
  commercially frozen, 27
  cooked in own juice, 122
  freezing, 21, 27–8, 122
  and Jelly Fillings, 132
  juices, 23
  Pie, Copenhagen, 150
  Salad, Fresh, 131
  Sponge Pudding, 146–7
  storage times, 23
  thawing, 33–4

Garlic, 24
Ginger
  Delights, 148
  Snaps, 144–5
Gobbets, Beef, 59
Gooseberries, 122
Goulash, Hungarian, 58

Haddock Filling, 102
Ham, left-over, 182
Hamburgers, 62
Harvard Beet, 114
Herbs, 28, 121
Hungarian
  Goulash, 58
  Lamb, 66

Ice Cream, 126–8
  Desserts, 128–9
  Economy, 127
  storage time, 23
  to serve, 34
  Toppings, 129–31
Italian Meat Sauce, 170

Jam Sponge Pudding, 146–7
Jellies, 28
Jelly and Fruit Fillings, 132

Kedgeree, 52
Kidney
  Filling, 102
  Pilaff, 99
  Rice Soufflé, 99
  à la Signorita, 77

Labelling, 19
Lamb
  Breast of Lamb Cutlets, 68
  Bredee (lamb stew), 65
  chops and cutlets, 27, 34
  freezing, 27
  Hungarian Lamb, 66
  Kidney Filling, 102
  Kidneys à la Signorita, 77
  Likky Frizzle (breast of lamb), 67
  à la Manchèga, 64
  roast, left-over, 182
  storage times, 23
  thawing, 34–5
Lard, storage time, 23
Lasagne, 100
Left-overs, 30, 181–2
  Casserole Filling, 101
  roast meat, 182
  in soup, 26, 47
  storage time, 23
Lemon
  Curd, Mock, 151
  sliced, 30
  Syrup, 130
Likky Frizzle (breast of lamb), 67
Liver
  and Bacon Filling, 103
  and Bacon Rice Soufflé, 99
  Cakes, 76
  Fried, 76
  Pilaff, 99
  raw frozen, 34
  storage time, 23

Madeira Cake, 139
Margarine, storage time, 23
Marmalade Sponge Pudding, 146–7
Marrow Casserole, 115
Mayonnaise, 24
  Canadian, 168
Meat and poultry
  freezing, 27
  storage times, 23
  thawing, 34–5, 36
  see also Beef; Chicken; Lamb; Pigeons; Pork; Veal; Venison
Meat Balls, Swedish, 63
Meat Sauce, Italian, 170
Meringue, soft, 24
Meringues Glacés, 129
Milk
  freezing, 29
  storage time, 23
  thawing, 35
Mince Minute Steaks, 60
Minute Steaks, 60
Moly Sauce, 155–6
Mushrooms
  Buttered, 114
  Filling, 101
Mustard Cream Sauce, 162

Nut
  Butterscotch Filling, 132
  Topping, 131

Omelettes, Savoury, 84
  Fillings, 101–4
Onion
  Rings, 116
  slices, frozen, 29–30, 107n
  and Tomato or Pimento Sauce, 164
Open freezing, 15, 19, 21
Orange
  Brandy Butterscotch Sauce, 130
  Cake, 139
  Cakes, Small, 137
  Delights, 148
  Syrup, 130

Packing
  materials, 17–19
  methods, 20–1
Pain de Gênes, 139
Pancakes, 97
  Cheese, 87
  Fillings, Savoury, 101–4
  Fillings, Sweet, 132–3
  Miniature, 98
  Sauces, Sweet, 129–30
  Sweet, 125
Parsnips, blanching and freezing, 107
Pasties, Cornish, 95–6
Pastry
  Cake Foundation, 150–1
  Cases, 157–60
  Flaky, 156
  freezing, 28, 152
  Puff, 153–6
  Rough Puff, 156
  Shortcrust, 152
  Slices, 160
  storage times, 23
  Sweet Shortcrust, 152–3
  Sweets made with, 124
  thawing, 36, 152
Peanut Nibbles, 145
Peas, blanching and freezing, 107
Pêche Melba, 129
Peppers, red or green, 29–30, 107
Perishable ingredients, 29–30
Pigeons with Mushrooms or Peppers, 82
Pilaff, Kidney or Liver, 99
Pimento and Onion Sauce, 164
Pineapple Plaisance, 147
Pizzas, 180
Polystyrene trays, 19
Polythene bags, 18
Pork
  Barbecued Spare Rib, 71
  Chinese Sliced, 70

Pork—*cont.*
chops, 27, 34
freezing, 27
Porc à la Fermière, 69
roast, left-over, 182
storage times, 23
thawing, 34–5
Potato
Bacon Cakes, 89
Cakes, 119
Croquettes, 117
Potatoes
Duchess, 118
Plain Mashed, 117
Sauté, 120
Poultry, *see* Chicken; Pigeons
Puddings and Sweets, 28, 123
using Cake Foundation, 146–50
Ice Cream, 126–8
Desserts, 128
made with Pancakes, 125
made with Pastry, 124
quickly served, 40
Sauces, Toppings and Fillings, 129–33
Puff Pastry, 153–6
Cases, 157
Slices, 124, 160
Vol-au-Vents, 158–60

Queen Cakes, 138
Quiche Lorraine, 92
Miniature, 93
Quickly served frozen dishes, 39–40

Raspberries, 122
Delights, 149
Shortcake, 149–50
Ratatouille, 108
Record keeping, 22
Red Cabbage, Braised, 109
Reheating frozen food, 30–8
Rice
Boiled, 104
Cakes, 138
freezing and thawing, 104–5
Fried, 105
Pilaff, 99
Soufflés, 99
Rolls, Bread, 176–7
Rough Puff Pastry, 156–7

Salad Dressing, French, 171
Salads, 24, 38, 120–1
Beetroot, 120
Cabbage, Braised Red, 109
Cabbage, Sweet and Sour, 110
Carrots, Buttered, 113
Celeriac, 121
Ratatouille, 108
Sandwich, Victoria, 135
Sandwiches, 28, 31
Cheese Foundation in, 89
Sauce
freezing, 29
storage time, 23
thawing, 37
Sauces, Savoury
Basic Rich White and Variations, 161–3
Cheese Cream, 163
Cheese Foundation, 163
Curry, 165
Curry Cream, 162
Drawn Butter, 166
Dutch, 168
Espagnol, 169
Italian Meat, 170
Moly, 165
Mustard Cream, 162
Onion and Tomato or Pimento, 164
Soubise, 163
Sweet Sour, 167
Tomato Cream, 167
Sauces, Sweet
Butterscotch and Variations, 129–30

Sauces, Sweet—*cont.*
Orange or Lemon Syrup, 130
Sausage
Pinwheels, 93
Rolls, 94
Sausages
Grilled, 93
storage time, 23
thawing, 34, 35
Scones, 141–2
Sealing materials, 19
Shortcrust
Biscuits, 144
General Purpose Pastry, 152
Sweet, 152–3
Shrewsbury Biscuits, 143
Slow Cooking Method, 44–6
casseroles, 44
food amenable to, 46
recipes suitable for, 47
Smothered Steak, 56
Soubise Sauce, 163
Soufflés, Rice, 99
Soup, 47
Creamy, made from left-overs, 48
freezing, 26
made from frozen sauces, 49
storage time, 23
thawing, 37
Spaghetti Bolognese, 99
Spare Rib, Barbecued, 71
Spice Butterscotch Sauce, 130
Spinach, blanching and freezing, 107
Sponge
Cakes, bought, 184
Cakes, Small, 136
Puddings, 146–7
Toppings for, 147
Standard, 136
Victoria, 135
Stacking, 21
Steak
Flemish Braised, 55
Mince Minute, 60
Minute, 60
Smothered, 56
Storage times, 22–3
Store-cupboard
Fillings, 104
Supplements, 183
Strawberries, 122
Delights, 149
Shortcake, 149–50
Sugar Biscuits, Continental, 144
Sultana Cake, 140
Surplus foods, freezing, 30, 181–2
Swedish Meat Balls, 63
Sweet and Sour
Cabbage, 110
Sauce, 167
Sweets, *see* Puddings and Sweets

Tartlet Cases, 157
Temperatures, 15
Thawing frozen foods, 30–8
Tinned foods
partly used, 181
to use with frozen dishes, 183–4
Toast, 28, 31
Tomato
Cream Sauce, 162
and Onion Sauce, 164
Tomatoes, freezing, 107n
Trays, freezer, 19
Treacle
Fruit Cake, 140
Sponge Pudding, 146–7
Trifle, 124, 184
Turnips, blanching and freezing, 107

Vacuum packed potatoes and vegetables, 184
Vanilla, 24
Veal
freezing, 27
Fricassée of, 73
with Mushrooms and Cream, 72
storage times, 23

Veal—*cont.*
  thawing, 34–5
  Wiener Schnitzel, 73
Vegetables
  blanching and freezing, 106–7
  Cabbage, Sweet and Sour, 110
  Carrots, Buttered, 113
  Celeriac
    Buttered, 113
    Purée, 113
    Salad, 121
    in Sauce, 112
  Celery
    à l'Italien, 111
    Rarebit, 87
  commercially frozen, 27, 106–8
  Courgette Casserole, 115
  Harvard Beet, 114
  Marrow Casserole, 115
  Mushrooms, Buttered, 114
  Onion Rings, 116
  Potato dishes, 117–20
  Ratatouille, 108
  Red Cabbage, Braised, 109
  with Rich White Sauce, 161
  Salads, 120–1
  storage times, 23
  thawing, 37–8
Venison, Pot Roast, 75
Victoria Sandwich, 135
Vienna Biscuits, 143
Vol-au-Vent
  Cases, 28, 158–60
  Fillings, 101–4

Weights and Measures, 43–4
Welsh Rarebit, 87
White Sauce, Basic Rich, 161
  Variations, 162–3
  with Vegetables, 161
Wiener Schnitzel, 73

Yeast, 175